The Homeplace
History and Receipt Book

History, Folklore, and Recipes
from Life on an Upper Southern Farm
a Decade before The Civil War

For Mary,
Blessings on your homeplace!

Geraldine Ann Marshall

Geraldine Ann Marshall
Sept 1, 2013

The Friends of Land Between The Lakes Publishing

Cookbook Project Coordinator

and Historical Consultant:

Cindy L. Earls

Recipe Consultant:

Charlotte Huggins

Illustrations:

Brooke Gilley and Michael W. Earls

Photographs:

Jennifer Lee Roberts

Publisher:

The Friends of Land Between The Lakes

345 Maintenance Road

Golden Pond, KY 42211

ISBN-13: 978-1480078932

ISBN-10: 148007893X

All photographs were taken at The Homeplace.

For information on The Homeplace, call 931-232-6457
or visit us at *www.lbl.org*

To my daughters, Audrey and Rachel

In memory of my grandmothers,
Audrey Marshall and Gramatula Zarvis

In memory of my sister of the heart, Lynn

G.A.M.

To my best friend and husband, Mike

To my parents, Nancy and Warren Manwiller
for their love and support

To my wonderful sons, Michael and Daniel

C.L.E.

Acknowledgments

All books create a community, but especially this book! Many thanks to Cindy and Charlotte for days of discussing ideas and recipes and all of their work. Thanks to Miss Scarlett's Restaurant for letting us spread out our papers and drink coffee through the day. Thanks to all of Friends of Land Between The Lakes and The Homeplace staff, past and present, for their knowledge. We are indebted to Sue Mathis for her recipe development, and appreciative of technical assistance and over 40 years of friendship from Mona Landrum Proctor. Thanks to Fain Russell for his patience and help as the author searched through old newspaper archives in two states!

G.A.M.

Special thanks to our female ancestors who <u>had</u> to prepare meals every day for their family. Their treasured family recipes that have been handed down to us are not only a list of ingredients; they are, in many ways, a record of their daily lives. Through their recipes, we can begin to understand their daily routine of hard work that provided food for their family from planting seeds to preparing a cake for a special occasion. The Homeplace's foodways program gives a voice to these women by preserving their story. We gain an appreciation of their work and begin to understand what it took to put a meal on the table.

Special thanks to the women interpreters who collected and experimented with period recipes to produce historical meals for the farmhouse dinner table. Many shared their family recipes with us new to the area. The living history women's program has evolved from the first opening of The Homeplace in 1978 and continues to do so. New research produces new period recipes and knowledge of historical preparation techniques. This book is a record of their work. Other foodlore and country recipes were shared by local families.

Special thanks to John Rufli, Director of Friends of Land Between The Lakes, Jim Taylor, Director of Operations of Friends of Land Between The Lakes, and Robert Holliday, The Homeplace Lead Interpreter, for believing in this project. And to Denise Schmittou, Belinda Gibson, and Emily Schmadeke for their technical assistance.

Special thanks to Gerry Ann Marshall and Charlotte Huggins, for without them this book would never have happened. Current interpreters and apprentices who contributed to this book include Jennifer Roberts, Ellen Bravard, Rebecca Wilson, and Jessye Bostwick.

C.L.E.

Contents

Recipe or Receipt

Both recipe and receipt come from the same Latin root, meaning to give. Receipt was often used by the British and tended to be used more often by Americans settlers; it was used in cookbooks through most of the nineteenth century.

Spelling and tense variations were common in Victorian literature. Such variations have been kept intact within quotations from books, journals and newspapers of that time.

Cooking ingredients change through time as does what is considered healthy for different conditions. If you are watching cholesterol levels and ratios, please feel free to use cooking sprays or oils, such as olive oil, for the lard and bacon grease called for in the recipes. As Sarah Josepha Hale said in the nineteenth century, "Bear in mind that in preparing food, three things are to be united, the promotion of health, the study of economy, and the gratification of taste."

Introduction

Welcome to The Homeplace

The Homeplace is a living history museum with sixteen original buildings, set in the 1850s, located in the Land Between The Lakes National Recreation Area in Kentucky and Tennessee. Original log houses, barns, cribs, heirloom crops and vegetables, heritage farm animals and historical interpreters create the sense of going back in time. Period-correct-costumed historical interpreters portray a yeoman (middle-class) family between the Cumberland and Tennessee River areas going about their daily chores that change with the seasons. The work of the day revolves around food production: plenty of food for their family and extra to sell.

The Historical Foodways program at The Homeplace was developed and continues to be refined by the women interpreters since the beginning of the living history museum. The foodways of a yeoman farm in upper middle Tennessee are extensively researched using primary and secondary sources. Period cookbooks give insight into the nineteenth-century foodways. Sharing of family receipts from former residents provide a closer look at the local foodways traditions. Diaries of farm women, although rare, allow us to step back in time to follow the lives of farm women depicted at The Homeplace. Through experimental archeology, interpreters gain valuable hands on experience learning skills in cooking and baking on wood stoves and hearth, using period gardening techniques and preservation of the farm raised-meats, vegetables, and fruit.

Come, join us at The Homeplace.

❖ *…Another year has sped by and I am spared to remain (on praying ground) where I hope I may improve my time and talent. Oh Lord I humbly pray for Grace to be enabled to do so. We have seen seven deaths during the year, and four births.*

~ December 31, 1859, Diary of Jane M. Jones

❖ *Mr. Gleaves has cider pressed. Commence the baby dress. Have peaches and cream.*

~ August 19, 1859, Diary of Betty Gleaves

As you exit the temperature-controlled Interpretive Center of The Homeplace and walk down the path, past the split rail fence, towards the Double Pen House, you have the rare chance to go back in time. Passing a field of open-pollinated heirloom corn, taking the stone steps up to the wooden porch of the house, imagine a woman such as Betty Gleaves sitting on the porch, stitching the baby dress, anticipating gathering her family for peaches and cream after dinner.

As you walk inside this house – or perhaps further into the farm, the Single Pen House – imagine a woman such as Jane M. Jones writing in her diary, praying for another year where her family will live through days when "Willie quite sick and dear little Mattie has a chill," (May 11, 1856) and she will stay well in order to do the work to keep her family well: "I am very busy sewing." (August 1, 1856); "I am all alone and hard at work. I made some catsup." (August 14, 1856); "Well I got up early and iced my cake. It looks very nice. All the young people came. I had a nice supper and then ice cream and fruit. Nearly all the young people staid all night. I got up early, had a nice breakfast. Never saw young people eat like they did." (August 12-13, 1856).

You have time-traveled back to the 1850s, the last decade before the Civil War (War Between the States) and arrived in the fertile land between the Cumberland and Tennessee Rivers. You have arrived in an area that both Kentucky and Tennessee claim at this time, but that will eventually become Tennessee. The nearby town of Dover, the county seat of Stewart County, is now a river trade center, the second largest steamboat port on the Cumberland River. Here and in other Tennessee and Kentucky towns, such as Clarksville, Eddyville, Canton, and Paducah, the family from The Homeplace can even find such goods as flour, lard, and bacon if they need supplies to tide them over until harvest or hog slaughtering. Such treats as Javanese or Brazilian coffee, refined cane sugar, tea, spices, chocolate, hard candy could be bought in the larger towns. For holidays, a family might purchase a block of aged New England cheddar cheese or English stilton instead of serving their own soft cheese. Those who did not ascribe to the budding temperance movement might consider buying whiskey, and rarely available European wines, brandies and West Indian rum. Yet luxuries would have been rare treats for the middle-class yeoman farm families in the 1850s.

Originally settled in the late 1700s to 1830s by sturdy folks of Scots Irish ancestry who arrived with only the basics of life: ax, livestock, horse, oven, pots, kettles, and household bedding, and built small cabins 16 to 17 feet long, little larger than a modern-day family room, The Homeplace area in the 1850s had what the original settlers might have considered an abundance. Those first settlers relied firstly on basic stores of bacon, salt, and cornmeal, consumed mostly cornmeal and pork, and foraged for wild plants and hunted for game to add mealtime variety.

So although consumer goods were available and larger homes had been built by the 1850s, The Homeplace family strove for as much self-sufficiency as possible. As history professor Donald L. Winters states in <u>Tennessee Farms, Tennessee Farming: Antebellum Agriculture in the Upper South</u>, "…providing for the household was traditional element of Tennessee farm life….many farmers were short of cash at certain times of the year….the scarcity of money encouraged families to provide as much as possible for the household needs from the farm…Their determination to meet family subsistence requirements was also part of a rural way of life that placed value on independence from the outside world."

As you visit The Homeplace, imagine you are part of the family. Your farm would be between 250 and 300 acres, and your entire family would work to cultivate around eighty acres. Slavery existed in the area and a yeoman farmer might aspire to own a slave, or might rent a slave from a local slave owner when possible, though a few farms in The Homeplace area did own slaves. Your family's yearly income would be between 100 and 200 dollars, earned by selling cash crops of tobacco, Indian corn, as well as livestock. A large majority of the work on the farm was directed toward providing food for the family and extra crops and livestock to sell for extra income.

Child, woman, or man, your help would be vital in making the farm succeed. You would know your environment well: know the signs for planting, read the sky for rain, and know when to collect wild plants for medicine, natural dyes, and food.

If you are a child, you would go to school sessions when your parents could do without your work on the farm, but you would mostly learn from working in farm and home with your family and neighbors. You might plow, plant, and hoe vegetables. If you are a boy, you might carry the water to your mother and sisters for the weekly clothes washday.

If you are a man, your work would consist of running the farm itself and doing much of the dealing with the outside world. Though you would do little women's work in these defined days, you would help where needed, especially with heavy household work, such as carrying water for doing laundry, moving large furniture when cleaning, and butchering large animals.

If you are a woman, your life - like that of Betty and Jane - would revolve around home and children. You would plow, plant, and hoe when needed in the fields. Much of your life though would be that of tending the family vegetable garden, to your children and husband, to those sick in your household. Harvesting the garden and preserving vegetables, fruits, and meats would be vital to your family's survival. You would make extra money for your family by selling extra eggs (even today, we know the term "egg money"), butter, and milk to local stores. Butter packed in brine or salt water could even be sent to cities such as Clarksville and Nashville. You would look forward to community gatherings for holidays, weddings, and work bees. Church and camp meetings would likely be a part of your life.

And you would spend much time tending hearth or stove. Receipts (recipes) would be a large part of your life. If you are one of the fortunate women who could read and write, you might have a cookbook such as Lettice Bryan's <u>Kentucky Housewife,</u> or Eliza Leslie's <u>Directions for Cookery in Its Various Branches</u>. You might even keep a written record of your receipts. If you, like many farmwomen at this time, cannot read or write, these receipts will be verbally taught to you from girlhood by mothers, grandmothers, aunts, and sisters. One of the first receipts you might learn is for the 1, 2, 3, 4 Cake. You will know what to do!

Follow the family of The Homeplace in the 1850s. Learn how the work and food changed with each season. Learn the cooking secrets of The Homeplace. Let's get ready to send those delightful dishes warm to the table and serve it up!

WINTER

❖ *Roads too bad and Frank lame. We go horseback.*
  Found all at Forest Hill Church. Uncle Sandy
  preached…..

      ~ January 31, 1859, Diary of Betty Gleaves

❖ *Today is my 25th birthday and Oh I do humbly pray*
  that I may serve the Lord anew.

      ~ February 5, 1857, Diary of Jane M. Jones

❖ *…On the 23 of December the ground froze and*
  remained so in places till first March. The coldest
  winter experienced for 36 years agreeable to my
  memory.

      ~ 1856, Diary of Samuel Stacker

With few fresh foods, especially green vegetables, The Homeplace family would have depended on their careful preparations for winter that provided salted, pickled, dried foods, and those few foods that could be stored for the winter.

While domesticated plants and animals were the main provisions of the farm family, farmers' diaries included hunting entries, especially in winter. Herndon Haraldson killed three deer in one day, forty-four ducks on another and twenty-two squirrels on another. John Barker bagged ten rabbits and twenty-four squirrels in one day!

What about canned foods? Though food was more likely to be preserved by salting, drying, or pickling in crocks until after the Civil War, the Mason jar, a boon to home canning, was patented by 1858. Commercially canned goods were also available, the first American patent for tin cans having been filed in 1839. By 1849, a machine had been invented that increased production of tin cans from five or six cans an hour to fifty to sixty cans per hour. Seafood, corn, tomatoes, and peas were sold commercially canned at this point. By 1856, Gail Borden had even received a patent for condensed milk. Steamboats coming into nearby landings, stores in such nearby cities as Clarksville, could have provided such occasional luxuries to families at The Homeplace.

Yet in winter, work included preparations for the next growing season. Winter plant beds were prepared by burning off old plants. Then tobacco seeds would be sown, as well as some summer food plants such as tomatoes, peppers, and cabbages. The plant beds were then covered with evergreens, protecting the new, tender plants from frosts and late freezes.

Beyond hard work, celebrations are a part of life and The Homeplace family too celebrated those days we celebrate today – and some days we have forgotten as well. Join in with the family with receipts for everyday fare (though you will just want to read about preparing red-birds while you watch the cardinals) and for special winter days.

Greeting the New Year

❖ *Brother Parish goes up to New Sharon. Mr. Gleaves goes with him. Jimmy McAninony came - very busy all day - make John a coat....*

~ Diary of Betty Gleaves, January 1, 1859

In her New Year's Day entry, Betty Gleaves doesn't detail her busy day beyond making a coat, but in much of the antebellum south New Year's dinner included a southern New Year's Day tradition of eating black-eyed peas, most likely with hog jowl or other pork, for luck.

Eating black-eyed peas on New Year's Day

is a must for good luck.

The peas should be eaten with pork, not chicken:

Hogs root forward with their noses,

while chickens scratch backwards.

On the New Year, it is time to move forwards!

~ Southern folklore

The tradition of eating black-eyed peas or other cow peas on the beginning day of a new year is an ancient tradition. How this good luck tradition reached The Homeplace and other homes in the south is a mystery, but we have the roots of possibility. In her book, <u>High on the Hog: A Culinary Journey from Africa to America,</u> food historian Jessica B. Harris says, "The black-eyed pea, which is actually more of a bean than a pea, was introduced into the West Indies from Central Africa in the early 1700s and journeyed from there into the Carolinas. The pea with the small black dot is considered especially lucky by many cultures in Western Africa. While the pea was certainly not lucky for those who were caught and sold into slavery, the memory of the luck it was supposed to bring in West Africa lingered on among the enslaved in the southern United States....(the black-eyed pea) consumed on New Year's Day by black and white Southerners alike is reputed to bring good fortune to all who eat it."

Many southern farm families have eaten some form of dried black-eyed peas (or other field peas) and salted pork on New Year's Day!

Good Luck Peas

6 cups water
1 pound (2 cups) any dried field pea
2 – 1 pound smoked ham hocks
    or 2 tablespoon bacon grease.
1 teaspoon salt
Pepper or crushed red pepper to taste

Soak the peas overnight in the water. Then, next day, add the ham hocks or bacon grease, salt and pepper to the peas. Bring to a boil over high heat, move to lower heat, and simmer gently two and one-half to three hours, or until the peas are very tender. When peas are done, remove ham hocks. Cut the meat from the bones, discard the skin, fat, and gristle, and cut the meat into small pieces.

Return the meat to the pot and take to table.

~ The Homeplace Recipe ~

Field Pea Soup

There are several kinds of field peas, some of which
are unfit for soup, being very dark; there are two kinds
that are white, and very nice for the purpose;
the one is large, and the other quite small,
being far the most delicate of this species.
They should be full grown, but not
the least hard or yellow.
Take three pints of either after they are hulled, rinse them clean,
and boil them with a small piece of pork or bacon. When they
are quite tender, take out the meat;
and if they are of the large kind of pea, mash a part of them, to
thicken the soup, but if they are small ones, do not break them,
as they look much prettier to serve whole.
There should be at least three pints of the liquor,
to which add four ounces of butter,
broken up and rolled in four tablespoonfuls of flour;
season it to your taste with salt and pepper, boil it up,
and then stir in gradually a pint of rich sweet cream,
and one and a half dozen of little force-meat balls,
    not larger than a nutmeg,
    made in the usual manner,
    and fried brown in butter.

~ Lettice Bryan, The Kentucky Housewife, 1839

Dried Bean Soup

Take the small white beans, which are nicest for this purpose,
hull them, and parboil them in clear water
till they begin to swell.
Then rinse them in clean water, and boil them till very tender,
with a piece of salt pork;
then take out the pork and the beans; mash the beans to a pulp,
and season it lightly with pepper;
mix with it an equal portion of boiled rice,
which has also been mashed fine;
make it into small balls or cakes; put over them the yolk of egg,
slightly beaten,
dust them with flour,
and spread them out on a cloth to dry a little.
Having seasoned the liquor with salt and pepper to your taste,
put in a large lump of butter, rolled in flour; boil it up,
stir in half a pint of sweet cream, and then put in
the cakes or balls. Serve it up
immediately, or they will dissolve,
and make the soup too thick. This is a plain, unexpensive soup,
but a very good one.

~ Lettice Bryan, <u>The Kentucky Housewife</u>, 1839

Good to serve with black-eyed peas or with beans are:

Homeplace Hoe Cakes

2 cups cornmeal
  (white is more traditional, but you can use yellow;
  stoneground is best)
1/2 teaspoon salt
1 cup boiling water
1 tablespoon bacon drippings
  (if you don't use drippings, olive oil will work)

Combine the cornmeal and salt in a mixing bowl. Stir in boiling water. Divide the mix into eight portions, shaping each into an approximately three inch (diameter) circle. In a skillet (cast iron if possible), heat the drippings until drops of water hop. Fry over medium heat, turning till brown. Serve warm!

~ The Homeplace Recipe ~

Hoe cakes get their name because they were first baked over a fire on the edge of a hoe. One old custom said that when a young man turned a hoe cake without breaking it, he was ready for marriage.

~ Southern folklore

In the 1850s, gem pans (instead of muffin tins) were often used. Generally made of cast iron, gem pans had a fluted design for each individual gem.

Cornmeal Gems

Makes two dozen

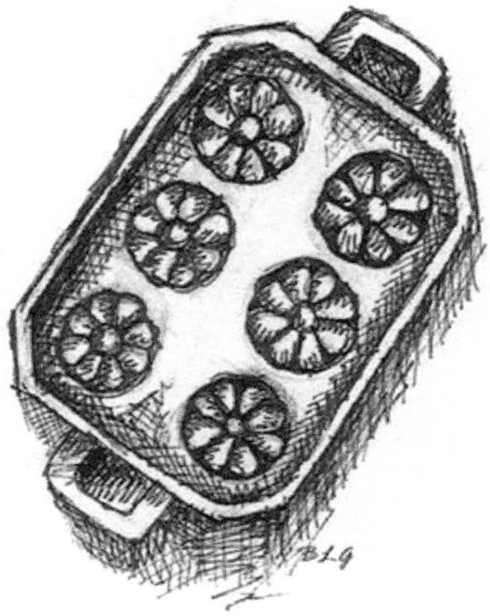

1 and 1/2 cups flour
3/4 cup cornmeal
1/4 cup sugar
1 tablespoon plus
    1 and 1/2
    teaspoons
    baking powder
1 teaspoon salt
1 egg, beaten
2/3 cup milk
1/3 cup butter, melted

Preheat oven to 375 degrees.

Combine flour, cornmeal, sugar, baking powder, and salt. Mix in a bowl. Combine egg, milk, and butter in another bowl. Add the liquid ingredients to the dry ingredients, stirring only enough to dampen all of the dry ingredients. Spoon batter into greased muffin cups or gem pan cups. Bake until gold brown fifteen to twenty muffins, until muffins are firm to the touch. Turn out upside down.

~ The Homeplace Recipe ~

New Year's Cookies

Rub to a cream 3/4 pound of butter and 1 pound of sugar and 3 well beaten eggs, 2 spoonfuls of caraway seed, a grated nutmeg, and 1 teaspoon saleratus (baking soda) dissolved in a teacup of milk and strained into half a teacup of cider. Add flour to make cookies stiff enough to roll out. As soon as cut into cakes, bake in a quick oven till of a light brown.

~ A.I. Webster, The Improved Housewife, 1858

From "A Dirge for the Dying Year"

The O'd Year's dying hour has come;

Let grief's pale shroud be cast

Around him - chant a requiem,

And leave him with the past.

And now, to deck the New Year's shire,

Go gather wisdom's flowers,

That wisdom's quenchless star may shine

Upon his parting hours.

Rosa

~ Published in The Clarksville Jeffersonian newspaper, February 8, 1854

The First Requisite Is to Have a Good Cow: Making Butter

As butter & eggs bear a good price I gather up all the eggs I can - fix my butter for Caleb to take Monday on the boat - butter is from 25 to 50 cents per pound 7 eggs 15 cts per dozen.

~ Diary of Betty Gleaves, January 8, 1859

"…No branch of household economy brings a better reward than the making of butter; and to one who takes an interest in domestic employments, it soon becomes a most pleasant occupation…. The first requisite is to have a good cow. One that has high hips, short fore-legs and a large udder is to be preferred. The cream-colored and the mouse-colored cows generally give a large quantity and of rich quality. Her feeding should be faithfully attended to. She should have a good pasture not far distant, or if this is impracticable, care must be taken that she is not made to run - a piece of mischief frequently practiced. Give her a teacup full of salt once a week. Feed her once a day the waste from the kitchen, adding to it about a pint of Indian meal. Give her the skimmed milk not wanted by the family. If she does not readily drink it, teach her by keeping her a few days without water. Take care that nothing is given her which will injure the taste of the milk, such as turnips and parsnips. Carrots are a fine vegetable for cows. Have her milked by a person who understands the process, or she will not give freely, and will soon become dry."

    ~ Mrs. M.H. Cornelius, <u>The Young Housekeeper's Friend</u>, 1846

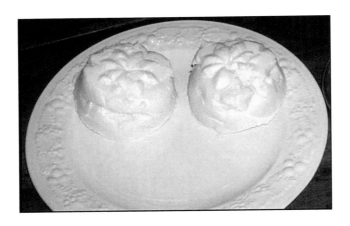

…The great requisites in preserving and making good butter are; 1st. That everything should be cleanly in the whole process. 2nd. That milk should be kept at a proper temperature, say from 45 degrees to 55 degrees, while the cream is separating. 3rd. That the cream should be taken off and churned before its quality is impaired. 4th. That its temperature should be from 55 degrees to 65 degrees when put into the churn, and the churning should be moderate and uniform. 5th. That salt, of the best quality (say alum salt made fine), in sufficient quantity to suit the palate, should be blended with it in the first working, and the buttermilk completely got out by the butter-ladle. 6th. That the working of the butter should be repeated at the end of twenty-four hours, when the salt has become completely dissolved, and all the liquid extracted. 7th. That it should be packed without more salt to make it weigh, in stone jars, in wooden firkins or tubs, such as will not impart to it any taint or bad flavour, and in such manner as will totally exclude the atmosphere.

Butter made in this way will be of fine flavour; and if put down and kept in this way, the flavour will be preserved to an almost indefinite period, if kept in a temperature below 70 degrees;...

~ Phineas Thornton, <u>The Southern Gardener and Receipt Book,</u> 1845

Come butter come,

Come butter come,

Peter standing at the gate

Waiting for a butter cake

Come butter come.

The above traditional chant from a Mother Goose rhyme became a work song for churning butter. The song was sung faster and faster after each verse as the churner chanted for the cream to become butter by pressing the dasher faster and faster. Traditionally, the dasher would be pressed down on "come" and pulled up on "butter."

Huzza! for General Jackson
Jackson Day, January 8

In her 1913 book, <u>Dishes and Beverages of the Old South</u>, Martha McCulloch-Williams, who recounted her memories and recipes from growing up in pre-Civil War Tennessee on a plantation near The Homeplace area, has left us a treasure trove of the customs and foods of this time. She refers to one of the "high" days as Jackson's Day - "the eighth of January."

The eighth of January was the anniversary of the 1815 Battle of New Orleans, in which Major General Andrew Jackson led his small army to victory against eight thousand British troops during the War of 1812, and made the future seventh president (Jackson was elected in 1828 and reelected in 1832) a national hero. Especially in the South in the nineteenth century, this anniversary was still a day for celebration. With his Tennessee homestead the Hermitage (near Nashville, Tennessee) and his similar Irish-Scotts heritage (Jackson was a native of North Carolina), surely some butter and eggs would've gone to commemorating Jackson Day. Those butter and eggs could have been used with the nuts from hickory trees, such as the shagbark hickories that grow around The Homeplace today.

With his nickname of "Old Hickory," attributing the toughness of hickory to the toughness of the man, when Jackson was inaugurated women wore necklaces of hickory nuts. It is also reported that Jackson liked foods with hickory nuts. Whatever your politics, past or present, Jackson Day is a good day to bake a hickory nut cake.

Hickorynut Cake

Two cupfuls sugar, two thirds cupful butter, three and one-half cupfuls flour, whites of 4 eggs well beaten, 3 tspns. Baking powder mixed with flour, one cupful sweet milk, 1 1/2 pints of sliced (not chopped) hickory nuts. This makes two rather small loaves.

~ Printed in nineteenth century newspaper

Further instructions to the modern cook: Bake the cake in a moderate (350 degree) oven for approximately thirty to forty-five minutes until a toothpick comes out clean. A woman at The Homeplace might have used a bent broom straw or a clean straw broken off from the near top part of the broom to test the cake for doneness.

It is unlikely that the women at The Homeplace would have had newfangled commercial baking powder. According to Greg Patent in his book, <u>Baking in America: Traditional and Contemporary Favorites from the Past 200 Years,</u> commercial baking powder "arrived in the late 1850s." Prior to baking powder, Patent says, "From the time <u>American Cookery</u> appeared in 1796 to the mid-1800s, American bakers showing a zest for saving time that continues to this day, experimented with various chemical leaveners. The first was pearlash (potassium carbonate), then came saleratus (sodium carbonate), then came baking soda (sodium bicarbonate)." Pearlash and saleratus are often referred to in 1800s cookbooks.

Walnut Cake

Hickory or other nuts can be used

2 cups brown sugar
1/2 cup butter, worked to a cream
3 eggs, beat separately
3/4 cup milk
2 1/2 cups flour, scant
1/2 cup walnuts, ground
2 teaspoon baking powder

Mix together and bake at 350.

Nut Cake Icing

1 cup white sugar
1 cup cream or top milk
1 cup nuts ground

Boil until thick enough to spread.

~ The Homeplace Recipe ~

Our States can of their freedom boast,

Although our foes should be a host,

We quick can drive them from our coast –

Fill up your glasses and drink a toast

T' the health of Gen'ral Jackson.

Remember New Orleans I say,

Where Jackson show'd them Yankee play,

And beat them off and gain'd the day,

And then we heard the people say

Huzza! for Gen'ral Jackson

~ from "Huzza! for General Jackson"
Nineteenth-century song sheet
Library of Congress

Drink a Toast to Health

❖ *There was great temperance speaker in town today,*
Mr. Phil White. I did not hear him. Everyone was
very much pleased with him.

~ March 8, 1850, Diary of Jane M. Jones

To Make Turnip Wine

Take a good many turnips, pare, slice and put them in a cider press, and press out all the juice very well. To every gallon of juice have three pounds of lump sugar, have a vessel ready just big enough to hold the juice, put your sugar into a vessel, and also to every gallon of juice, half a pint of brandy. Pour in the juice and lay something over the bung for a week, to see if works. If it does, you must bung it down till it has done working; then stop it closed for three months and draw it off in another vessel. When it is fine, bottle it off.

~ From collection of nineteenth-century cookbooks ~
in the Hermitage library

Sassafras Mead

Mix gradually, with two quarts boiling water, three and a half pounds of best brown sugar, a pint and a half of good molasses, and one fourth of a pound of tartaric acid, stir it well, and when cool strain it into a large jug, or pan, then mix in a quarter of an ounce of essence of sassafras; transfer it to clean bottles, (it will fill about half a dozen), cork it tightly and keep it in a cool place.

Have ready a box containing about one fourth of a pound carbonate of soda to use with it. To prepare a glass of it for drinking, pour a little of the mead into a tumbler, fill three-fourths full of cold water, then stir in a small quantity of soda and it will foam to the top.

~ Esther Allen Howland,
The American Economical Housekeeper and Family Receipt Book,
1850

Cordial Peppermint

Take spirit of wine two ounces; English oil of peppermint, half an ounce; mix them together; then add the spirit to a syrup made by boiling lump sugar, two pounds, in one gallon of water: good for flatulence, and to prevent the griping of aperient medicines.

~ Godey's Lady's Book, October 1859

Everyday Fare

In her book, <u>A Taste of Kentucky</u>, Janet Alm Anderson quotes Mrs. Wills about drying green beans "that wound around a cornstalk." Instructions are:

"You wash them, then you string them and dry them in the sun. Then you take a needle (darning needle type) and a piece of twine and string them up. Then hang them in the sun or close to heat."

According to Bill Best in <u>The Southern Foodways Alliance Community Cookbook</u>, dried beans were called "shuck beans, shucky beans, leather britches…"

Leather Britches Beans

2 cups dried green beans
10 cups water
1/2 dried red pepper pod
(or 1/2 teaspoon red pepper)
Piece of smoked hog jowl or 3 slices of thick bacon

Soak the dried beans in a 4 quart saucepan (or larger) in 6 cups of water overnight. Pour off the water in the morning. Add the red pepper and the pork (jowl or bacon) and 4 cups of water to the beans. Bring to a boil, reduce heat, and cover. For dried beans, simmer for 2-3 hours (1 hour is enough for frozen beans), checking for tenderness. Add water if needed. Remove pork, or cut up and serve in the beans if you love it like I do!

~ The Homeplace Recipe ~

Saleratus (Soda) Biscuit

Makes about 16 biscuits

2 cups all-purpose flour
1 teaspoon baking soda
1/2 teaspoon salt
1/3 cup lard
3/4 cup buttermilk

Preheat the oven to 425°.

Stir the flour, baking soda, and salt together in a deep bowl. Add the lard, and with the tips of your fingers, rub the fat and the flour together until they resemble flakes of course meal. Pour in the buttermilk all at once and stir just long enough to combine it with the dry ingredients.

Gather the dough into a ball and put it on a lightly floured surface. Knead two or three times, until the dough is smooth and soft and hangs together well. Pat into a rough circle about one/half inch thick. With a two-inch biscuit cutter, cut the dough into rounds.

Arrange the rounds with edges touching on an ungreased baking sheet and bake in the middle of the oven for twelve to fifteen minutes until they are golden brown and crusty on top. Serve at once.

~ The Homeplace Recipe ~

In 1850, the cook relied upon saleratus or pearlash to leaven biscuits and other quickbreads. Saleratus, an early form of baking soda, and pearlash, a purified form of potash, both acted in combination with sour milk or buttermilk to release the carbon dioxide which caused the dough to rise. Earlier times on the frontier found the cook adding a pinch of lye to raise the biscuit. Today baking soda is substituted for saleratus.

Winter Sauerkraut

6 servings

2 tablespoons bacon drippings
  (substitute olive oil if desired)
1/2 cup onion, chopped
2 medium apples, peeled, cored, sliced
2 cups sauerkraut
1 cup water
1 teaspoon salt
1 tablespoon brown sugar
2 medium potatoes, peeled (if desired) and quartered

Cook onion in large skillet, stirring, until translucent. Add apples, potatoes, sauerkraut, water, sugar and salt. Cover and simmer 15-20 minutes until potatoes are tender.

~ The Homeplace Recipe ~

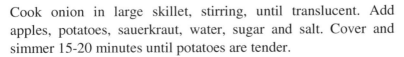

Winter Squash (cushaw)

This is much finer than the summer squash. It is fit to eat in August, and in a dry warm place, can be kept well all winter. The color is very bright yellow. Pare it, take out the seeds, cut it in pieces and stew it slowly, until quite soft, in a very little water. Afterwards, drain, squeeze, and press it well and mash it with a little butter, pepper, and salt.

~ Eliza Leslie, <u>Directions for Cookery, in its Various Branches</u>, 1848

Excellent Cold Slaw

Take a nice fresh white cabbage, wash, drain, and cut off the stalk. Shave down the head evenly and nicely into very small shreds, with cabbage cutter or a sharp knife. Put in a deep dish and prepare for it the following dressing. Take a jill or half-tumblerful of the best cider vinegar, and mix with it a quarter of a pound of fresh butter, divided into four bits, and rolled in flour and small salt-spoon of salt and the same quantity of cayenne. Stir well, and boil it in a small saucepan. Have ready the yolks of three eggs well beaten. As soon as the mixture has come to a hard boil, take it off the fire, and stir in the beaten egg. Pour it hot over the shredded cabbage and mix well all through, with a spoon. Set it to cool on ice or snow, or in the open air. It should be quite cold before going to table.

~ Eliza Leslie, <u>Directions for Cookery, in its Various Branches</u>, 1848

Ham and Cabbage

6 servings

Country ham (or city ham if you must),
   one pound, cut into 1 inch cubes
2 medium potatoes, peeled, cut into 1 inch chunks
1 medium cabbage, cored, and cut into 4 wedges
1/4 cup vinegar (I like apple cider vinegar)
1 cup water
1 teaspoon brown sugar
1 teaspoon salt
1/4 teaspoon black pepper (or pepper to your taste)

With ham fat, rub bottom of an iron skillet and heat until hot. Add the ham pieces, sear on each side, cook for about five minutes while stirring. Reduce heat to moderate. Add cabbage and 1/2 cup water. Cook for ten minutes, stirring, until cabbage is wilted. Add potatoes, vinegar, 1/2 cup water, brown sugar, salt and pepper. Cover and simmer 45 minutes, checking occasionally, until potatoes are tender.

~ The Homeplace Recipe ~

As the above recipes show, cabbages pickled into sauerkraut or otherwise preserved, were a sturdy winter vegetable. Potatoes were another hardy vegetable.

Making Bacon

This is the season for "curing hams," as some call the process of making bacon.

Everybody knows how to make bacon, and but very few succeed in making that which is good. A writer, over the signature of "H.M," in the last Farmer's Cabinet, remarks that "to cure hams thoroughly, so as to have them sufficiently salt to keep, and not too salt, and to give them the real *Jersey* flavor, is a delicate operation, and requires a nice hand. The following recipe is a good one, and may be relied upon for making a first rate ham: To 80lbs. of hams take four ounces of brown sugar, three ounces of saltpeter, and one pint of fine salt; pulverize and mix them thoroughly; rub the hams well all over, particularly on the flesh side, and lay them on boards for 36 to 48 hours; then pack them in casks, adding two quarts of fine salt to every 80 lbs. of hams. In fifteen or eighteen days they may be hung up to smoke."

The same writer says six lbs. of fine salt, four ounces of saltpetre, one and a quarter lbs. of brown sugar, make a good proportion for 100 lbs. of beef. In twenty-four hours a pickle that will bear an egg endways should be applied.

~ Southern Cultivator, Vol V No 3, March 1847

The 'pickle' in the above recipe refers to a salt brine.

Sausages

Proportion your meat about half fat and half lean; cut it fine; then to one hundred pounds of meat add two and a quarter pounds of salt, ten ounces sage, and ten ounces of pepper made fine. Warm the meat, and mix them in thoroughly and stuff them, and the thing is done right. If any wish to keep them through the summer good and fresh, put them in a clean firkin, warm fat and pour in until you cover them; cover and set them in the cellar, and they will keep good the year round.

~ Southern Cultivator, Vol V No 5, May 1847

Beet Pickles

4 pounds small beets (about 20 beets)
2 cups granulated white sugar
2 cups apple cider vinegar
6 cups water
6 whole cloves
1-1 1/2 inch stick cinnamon

Trim the stems and the green tops from the beets, and scrub them clean under running water, being careful not to cut into the outer skin. Place the beets in a four to six quart kettle, add the water, and bring to a boil over high heat. Reduce the heat and simmer for thirty to forty minutes, or until the beets are tender.

Drain the beets, saving one cup of the liquid in which they were boiled, and set them aside to cool. Return the one cup of beet liquid to the kettle and add the sugar and the vinegar. Bring to a boil over high heat and boil briskly for five minutes.

Peel the beets and cut them into slices about 1/8 inch thick. Add the beet slices to the kettle, bring to boil again, lower the heat, and simmer for 15 minutes.

Transfer the slices into hot, sterilized Mason-type canning jars, adding one clove and one one-fourth inch piece of stick cinnamon to each jar. Fill the jars with the hot vinegar mixture to one-fourth inch from the top rim. Seal immediately, following the manufacturer's instructions for processing. Let the beets pickle in a cool, dark place for at least two weeks before serving.

~ The Homeplace Recipe ~

Pickled beets are freshly cooked beats served with a vinegar sauce. Beet pickles are what the women at The Homeplace made to serve with a winter dinner. The beet pickles would have been prepared in summer and stored in stoneware crocks for use in winter.

We have just received per steams T C. Twitchel and E. Howard the finest lot of

Groceries Ever brought to this market, which we are now selling cheaper than any other house in Providence or Clarksville. Our stock comprises the following articles -

25 hdds choice Sugar [hogshead]

13 hhds common Sugar [barrels]

75 sacks Rio Coffee

15 sacks …Java

…..

10 bbls Molasses

25 half bbls Molasses

…..

25 bbl Clover Seed

100 boxes Star Candies

12 box boxes Cheese

100 kegs Nails

And everything else usually kept in a Grocery which we will again say, we sell cheaper than the cheapest. All we want is a chance to prove what we say.

RADFORD & McGUIRE

Linwood Landing, Tenn.

~ People's Press newspaper, February 3, 1859
Christian County, Kentucky

Game Receipts

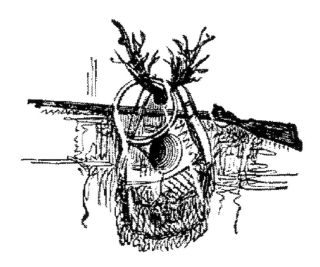

At The Homeplace, game would have been a welcome addition to dinner. In <u>Tennessee Farming, Tennessee Farmers: Antebellum Agriculture in the Early South</u>, Donald L. Winters emphasizes that: "Domesticated plants and animals were the family's primary source of nourishment. But the forest and streams supplemented the food produced on the farm and added variety to the household fare. Most of the buffalo had either migrated west or been killed by Indians before the arrival of the first immigrants. Early settlers hunted the few that remained in the western half of the state. Deer, rabbits, squirrels, ducks, turkeys, and boars were a more abundant source of wild meat. Farmers' diaries included references to hunting throughout the year, but especially in the winter months."

To Dress Red-birds,
or Any Sort of Small Birds

Rub the birds inside with a little salt, and put into each
a spoonful of grated ham,
a minced oyster,
or a lump of butter rolled in bread crumbs
and seasoned with pepper and nutmeg:
rub a little lard or butter over them,
and roast them before a brisk fire:
ten or fifteen minutes
will be quite long enough to roast them well.
Serve them upon small buttered toasts,
the edges of which having been neatly scalloped;
Pour over them the trail,
with a few spoonfuls of drawn butter, and lay on top of each bird
a broken bit of orange jelly
or a slice of ripe fruit.

~ Lettice Bryan, The Kentucky Housewife, 1839

Squirrel Soup

Take two fat young squirrels, skin and clean them nicely,
cut them into small pieces,
rinse and season them with salt and pepper,
and boil them till nearly done.
Beat an egg very light, stir it into half a pint of sweet milk,
add a little salt,
and enough flour to make it a stiff batter, and
drop it by small spoonfuls into the soup, and
boil them with squirrels till all are done. Then
stir in a small lump of butter,
rolled in flour,
a little grated parsley and half a pint of sweet cream;
stir till it comes to a boil, and serve it up
with some of the nicest pieces of the squirrels.
Soup may be made in this manner of small chickens,
pigeons, partridges, and pheasants.

~ Lettice Bryan, The Kentucky Housewife, 1839

Broiled Squirrels

Case and clean two fat young squirrels,
(old ones will not do;)
split them open on the back,
rinse them very clean in cold water,
season them with salt, pepper,
and grated lemon;
broil them on a gridiron, over clear coals, turning and basting
them two or three times with butter. When they are well done,
place them in a warm dish, sprinkle on them a handful
of grated bread, and pour over them two ounces of drawn butter.

~ Lettice Bryan, The Kentucky Housewife, 1839

To Fry Rabbits

Disjoint or cut them into small pieces, rinse them in cold water,
season them with salt, pepper and grated nutmeg,
dip them in a thin flour batter,
and fry them brown in boiling lard;
transfer them to a warm dish by the fire, stir in gravy
a handful of chopped parsley,
a spoonful of flour, and
a glass of sweet cream. Just stir it up
and pour it at once over the rabbits.

~ Lettice Bryan, The Kentucky Housewife, 1839

Venison Soup

Your venison must be quite fresh, as it is not fit for soup after the first five days. If it is a small one, take a whole shoulder, but if large, half a one will do. Chop it into several pieces, rinse them clean, and season them well with salt and pepper. Slice up a pound of ham, put it with the venison into a porridge pot; pour in enough water to cover the meat, add one or two sliced onions and a bunch of parsley, and boil it fast for a few minutes till scum rises; then remove the scum, cover the pot, and boil it gently till the meat is done very tender; after which take out the meat, reserve some of the nicest pieces to serve whole with the soup; mince from the bones a small portion of the other venison, and pound it in a mortar to a paste, adding

a teaspoonful of celery seeds, one of mace, lemon, and cloves,
half a one of cayenne, and by degrees a glass of red wine.
Strain the liquid into a soup-pan, and put in two ounces of butter,
rolled in flour; mix the beaten yolks of two eggs
in half a pint of entire sweet milk, and stir it in the soup;
add the venison paste, stirring by degrees: and before
it comes to a hard boil, serve it up;
put in a few small pieces of reserved venison,
and send it hot to table,
with a plate of dry toasts and a dish of boiled rice,
as both are much liked with venison soup.

~ Lettice Bryan, <u>The Kentucky Housewife</u>, 1839

Possum Roasted

Chill thoroughly after scraping and drawing. Save all the inside fat, let it soak in weak salt water until cooking time, then rinse it well, and partly try it out in the pan before putting in the possum. Unless he is huge, leave him whole, skewering him flat, and laying him skin side up in the pan. Set in a hot oven and cook until crisply tender, taking care there is no scorching. Roast a dozen good sized sweet potatoes - in ashes if possible, if not, bake them covered in a deep pan. Peel when done, and lay while hot around the possum, turning them over and over in the abundant gravy. He should have been lightly salted when hung up, and fully seasoned, with salt, pepper, and a trifle of mustard, when put down to cook. Dish him in a big platter, lay the potatoes, which should be partly browned, around him, add a little boiling water to the pan, shake well around, and pour the gravy over everything. Hot corn bread, strong black coffee, or else sharp cider, and very hot pickles are the things to serve with him.

~ Martha McCulloch-Williams, <u>Dishes & Beverages of the Old South</u>, 1913

Making a Quilt or Courting the Muses:
Valentine's Day

❖ *"Sister and myself have commenced her silk Quilt.
We are making it box work."*

~ Diary of Jane M. Jones, February 14, 1859

Next Tuesday is St. Valentine's Day. - From time "whereof the memory of man runneth not to the contrary," it has been celebrated as a day upon which the young folks select "companions" for the future. As we have already made our selection, the day will possess but little interest for us. Those who are not so fortunate would do well to court the muses, and see what can be done in the way of rhyming - and then call at C.O. Faxon's and procure an delicate and beautiful missive upon which to indite it. - He has an elegant assortment.

~ The Clarksville Jeffersonian newspaper, February 8, 1854

A folk belief from Britain was that birds chose their mates on Valentine's Day. Such a day was made for courtship! Valentine's Day notes had been written on writing paper since at least the 1700s, and by the 1820s, special paper for Valentine's Day was sold by such printers as C.O. Faxon advertising in <u>The Clarksville Jeffersonian.</u>

Actual Valentine's Day cards could also be bought as Esther Howland had started the New England Valentine Company in 1849 in Worchester, Massachusetts. Not everyone thought these courtship poems were such a lovely custom as the following editorial indicates:

Our beaux and belles are satisfied with a few miserable lines, neatly written upon fine paper, or else they purchase a printed Valentine with verses ready made, some of which are costly, and many of which are cheap and indecent.

In any case, whether decent or indecent, they only please the silly and give the vicious an opportunity to develop their propensities, and place them, anonymously, before the comparatively virtuous. The custom with us has no useful feature, and the sooner it is abolished the better.

~ <u>New York Times</u>, February 14, 1856

Whether or not any of those beaux and belles bought any actual cards or visited C.O. Faxon for a "delicate and beautiful" missive, the courtship food customs, likely helped out by the mothers of The Homeplace family (taking time from quilt-making and other household chores), surely would have found a sweet spot in anyone's heart.

Courtships

Write a variety of questions, each comprising one verse,
to which write many answers, and cut them apart.
Have ready sugar-plums of various kinds;
wrap a verse round each plum,
taking care not to mix them.
Take two kinds of glazed paper,
taking care to put questions in one color
and answers in another;
then twist the papers round the plums, under the curls,
which press back with your fingers,
so that they may entirely envelope the plums.
They should be handed round together,
that each one may have a solicitation with an answer,
in which lies the amusement, some answers
differing so far in sense to the subject of the questions.
This appears very simple to be sure, but it is quite amusing
to young people, for whom it is designed.

~ Lettice Bryan, The Kentucky Housewife, 1839

Kisses and Secrets

Beat the white of six eggs to a stiff froth,
add the juice of an orange or lemon,
and stir it into powdered loaf sugar, a little at a time,
till it is of the consistence of thick dough,
adding a very little starch.
Have ready some small paper cases,
about three quarters of an inch square,
put some buttered paper on tin sheets, lay on them the cases,
drop in each
a large tea-spoonful of the sugar and egg, make them smooth,
and bake them for a few minutes in a moderate oven;
then take them out of the cases,
wrap around each a slip of paper containing a single verse
or pun, and envelope them separately in small pieces of fine
white paper that is neatly fringed, giving each end a twist.

~ Lettice Bryan, The Kentucky Housewife, 1839

To get a hint of her companion - or fate - for the future, at
midnight, a girl walked around a peach tree, saying:

Low for a foreigner,
Bark for a near one,
Crow for a farmer.
Creak, tree, creak, if I am to die first.

~ Southern folklore

Peach Butter

Peach butter, when made in the proper manner, is cheap and really fine. Take cider just from the press, that has been made of the best of apples, boil it in a preserving kettle till reduced to one half its original quantity. Have ready made some nice dried peaches, wash them clean, squeeze out the water, and put them in the cider. Boil them till they are very soft, stirring them and mashing them till they become smooth pulp, and replenishing the kettle with fresh cider as it may require. Let it remain over a slow fire of coals till it gets hard enough to slice, but be careful to stir it almost constantly towards the last, lest it scorch. Flavor it highly with powdered cloves, ginger, cinnamon and nutmeg, put it up in stone of queen's ware jars, cover them securely by tying over the tops some folded paper, and keep them in a cool place. It will keep good a year, and will be found very nice and convenient.

~ Lettice Bryan, The Kentucky Housewife, 1839

At The Homeplace, heritage peaches are still grown. No matter what the peach tree told about the future in February, The Homeplace family would have been glad in winter for these preserved peaches!

Special Dinners

Old hens would have been culled in winter and used for dinner, leaving the young birds to produce more eggs and chicks in spring.

Chicken and Dumplings

Note: In this local recipe, the dumplings are like noodles. Local family tradition is to serve with cornbread dressing.

1 large old fat
    stewing hen
2 cups flour
2 tablespoon lard
    or shortening
1/2 cup cold water
    or cold chicken
    broth
Salt and black
    pepper to taste

In a large kettle, boil a stewing hen (old fat hen) till tender; add salt and black pepper to taste. Cook until meat falls off the bone, set aside to cool. Put about two cups of plain flour in a large mixing bowl, add salt and black pepper to taste. Cut in about two tablespoon of lard or shortening. Mix enough cold water or cooled chicken broth to make a good dough. Put a lot of flour on your cutting surface and also flour your rolling pen. Roll the dough out about to 1/4 to 1/8 of inch. Then cut with knife into 1 inch to 1 1/2 x 4 inch stripes or cut 3 x 3 inch square dumplings. Cover the dumplings in flour: they can sit for a while. Take the meat off the bones and put it back in broth, bring broth to boil. Drop the dumplings into boiling water, one at a time. As the pot fills with dumplings, gently move the dumplings around so that you have room for more dumplings.

DO NOT STIR THE DUMPLINGS.

Allow the dumplings to boil for a few minutes until they are well cooked. Then turn temperature down and allow cook slowly until the broth thickens, stirring occasionally. When broth thickens, cover the kettle, turn down the heat to keep warm and allow the chicken and dumplings to rest before serving. If dumplings fall apart, too much lard or shortening was added. If they are tough, not enough lard was added.

~ The Homeplace Recipe ~

Cornbread Dressing

cold cornbread (leftover)
1 medium onion chopped
salt, pepper, sage to taste

Crumble cornbread in large bowl, add broth enough to make mixture soggy, add onion and spices, put into skillet or baking dish. Place in oven at 400 degrees, bake until heated and browned.

~ The Homeplace Recipe ~

Chicken and Rice

One nice hen cut into parts. Brown hen in a little lard or butter with chopped onions and green peppers if desired. Pour 1 cup of rice into pot, place browned chicken and drippings into the pot and add 2 cups water or chicken broth. Bake in a moderate oven for about 1 hour making sure to check it for dryness. If getting dry add more water or broth.

~ The Homeplace Recipe ~

Raised Doughnuts

1 tablespoon yeast
2 tablespoons warm water
1/2 cup sugar
1 egg
1 cup warm milk
2 tablespoons melted butter
1/2 teaspoon salt
3 3/4 cup flour
Lard for deep frying
Sugar for coating (optional)

Put yeast, sugar, water, in a bowl and stir. Let proof ten to fifteen minutes. (Before quick acting yeast, yeast was proofed insuring that the yeast culture was alive and active.) Stir in egg, milk, butter, flour, and salt until springy. Lightly flour your fingers. Knead dough until soft, four to five minutes, or until the dough is soft and smooth and doesn't stick to your fingers or bowl. Place dough in warm place and let raise until it has double in size. When doubled in size, punch down and turn out on a floured cutting board. Roll one-half of the dough to one-half inch thickness and cut with doughnut cutter. Place cut doughnuts on platter or plate, warm until doubled again. Heat two inches of lard in a kettle until hot. Put doughnuts in heated lard a few at a time. Brown one side then turn to the other to brown. Drain. Sprinkle or roll in sugar, if desired.

~ The Homeplace Recipe ~

Flannel Cakes

Two pounds of flour, six eggs well beaten, one wineglass of yeast, a little salt, wet with milk into a thick batter, and set it to rise. Bake them in small pans.

~ Phineas Thornton, <u>The Southern Gardener and Receipt Book</u>, 1845

Dried Apple Cake

1 cup dried apples
1 cup molasses
1 tablespoon butter
1 3/4 cup flour
2 teaspoons soda
1/2 teaspoons cloves
1 teaspoons cinnamon
1/2 teaspoons salt
2/3 cup sour cream
1 cup brown sugar
1 egg

Put apples in a bowl and pour in enough cold water to cover. Let stand several hours or overnight. Chop apples finely, put in 1 1/2 to 2 quart pan and pour in the molasses. Bring to a boil over moderate heat and simmer twenty minutes. Let cool. With the butter grease the bottom and sides of skillet, dust with flour. Stir together flour, soda, spices, and salt, set aside. Combine sour cream, sugar, and egg in a large bowl and stir till smooth. Add the dry ingredients, 1/2 cup at a time and stir till mixed well. Pour in the molasses mixture and blend till smooth. Pour into prepared pan. Bake in a moderate oven for fifty to sixty minutes or until cake has begun to shrink form the sides of the pan.

~ The Homeplace Recipe ~

Pie Paste (to make pie crust)

One Crust:

1 1/2 cup flour
1/4 cup lard
1/4 cup butter
3-4 tablespoons cold water

Two Crust:

2 cups flour
1/3 cup lard
1/3 cup butter
4-6 tablespoons cold water

Combine flour, butter, lard, in a large mixing bowl. Cut lard and butter into flour till the mixture resembles small green peas. Add water one tablespoon at a time, until consistency is right and form into a ball. Flour well surface of dough board and rolling pin. Roll out.

~ The Homeplace Recipe ~

Fried Fruit Pies

Make a good pie paste. Roll out onto a well floured surface, very thin. Take a saucer plate, lay on paste, and cut out a circle. Have a skillet of bubbling lard on stove. Fill the pie paste circle with about one-fourth cooked fruit; lower pie into lard. Brown on both sides but don't burn.

~ The Homeplace Recipe ~

Half-Moon Pies

Pie paste for a double crust pie
3 cups dried peaches or other prepared fruit
2 cups boiling water
1/2 cup brown sugar
1/2 teaspoon cinnamon
1/2 teaspoon nutmeg
lard for frying

Cover the peaches with boiling water in a 2 1/2 to 3 quart pan and set aside for one-half hour. Then bring the water to boil; then simmer for twenty to twenty-five minutes until the peaches are tender and plump. Remove the pan from the heat, stir in the sugar and spices, and let cool. Drain the peaches and chop them coarsely. Halve the pie paste, roll out each half about 1/8 inch thick on a floured surface, and from each half cut about 12 rounds with a floured 4 1/2 inch cutter or small plate. Fill each round with a heaping tablespoon of the filling, brush the edges of the pie paste with water, and fold over to form half circles. Press edges together and seal with a fork. Fry the pies, three or four at a time, in a skillet filled two to three inches with hot lard, turning them once or twice, for four to five minutes until golden brown. Drain.

~ The Homeplace Recipe ~

Applesauce Spice Cake

1 1/4 cup flour
1 cup sugar
1 teaspoon soda
1/2 teaspoon salt
1/2 teaspoon cinnamon
1/4 teaspoon cloves
1/4 teaspoon allspice
1/16 teaspoon cream of tartar
3/4 to 1 cup applesauce
1/4 cup water
1/4 cup butter
1 egg
1/2 cup raisins (optional)
1/4 cup chopped nuts of your choice (optional)

Mix all the ingredients well. Pour into a well-greased loaf pan or nine-inch iron skillet. Bake in moderate oven (350 degrees) for about forty to fifty minutes. If the cake starts to brown too quickly, place a tin plate over top. Sprinkle with powdered sugar or a mixture of brown sugar, cinnamon, and plain white sugar.

~ The Homeplace Recipe ~

George Washington's Birthday

February 22

❖ *Sister Mary and myself walk up to church--a tolerable good sermon at the Methodist church.*

~ Diary of Jane M. Jones, February 22, 1857

❖ *Knitting...a collar, the crochet stitch...men went out on town. Some of them were so drunk they fell off their horses. Oh! So distressing.*

~ Diary of Betty Gleaves, February 23, 1858

 During the 1800s, the birthday of the first president of the United States, George Washington, was a national celebration! In cities, balls, teas and fireworks were popular. The occasion at The Homeplace was not so grand, but perhaps that sermon discussed the honesty and courage of the father of our country, and those men falling off the horses might have celebrated a little too much!

What better way to celebrate George Washington's birthday than to start out with a breakfast cake and continue on with cake from dinner to supper?

Washington Cake

(For breakfast)

This cake derives its name from the fact that it was a great favorite at the table of George Washington; the last two years of his life, it always formed one of the delicacies of his breakfast-table, and is considered one of the standing dishes of a Virginian.

Take two pounds of flour, one quart of milk, with an ounce of butter, heated together; put the milk and butter into the flour when it is about lukewarm, add one gill of good yeast, three eggs, a teaspoonful of salt, place it in pans over night, and bake it in the morning in a quick oven for three-quarters of an hour.

~ Phineas Thornton, The Southern Gardener and Receipt Book, 1845

(For the rest of the day and beyond)

WASHINGTON CAKE – Stir together a pound of butter and a pound of sugar; and sift into another pan a pound of flour. Beat six eggs very light, and stir them into the butter and sugar, alternately with the flour and a pint of rich milk or cream; if the milk is sour it will be no disadvantage. Add a glass of wine, a glass of brandy, a powdered nutmeg, and a tablespoonful of powdered cinnamon. Lastly, sift in a small teaspoonful of pearlash, or saleratus, that has been melted in a little vinegar; take care not to put in too much pearlash, lest it give the cake an unpleasant taste. Stir the whole very hard; put it into a buttered tin pan (or into little tins), and bake it in a brisk oven. Wrapped in a thick cloth, this cake will keep soft for a week.

~ Eliza Leslie, Directions for Cookery, in its Various Branches, 1848

Washington's Cake

Dissolve a teaspoonful of saleratus in a small
tea-cup-ful of boiling water,
let it set by the fire a few minutes,
and stir in three gills of butter-milk.
Beat to a cream a pound of butter
and a pound of powdered sugar,
And mix them with the water. Add a glass of white wine
and two powdered nutmegs;
and then stir in alternately six beaten eggs
and eighteen ounces of flour.
Stir it till well mixed and very smooth,
Put it in a buttered square pan, and bake it in a moderate oven.

~ Lettice Bryan, The Kentucky Housewife, 1839

Some Washington cakes included dried fruits, such as raisins. In George Washington's day these cakes were called great cakes or excellent cakes, but by the Victorian 1850s, such cakes were generally called fruit cakes. Such cakes were even being served at the beginning of the new year, as well as on Washington's Birthday.

Though it would have been rare for a Homeplace family to splurge on a confection, confectionary shops were available in the area and would have been patronized for community events for very special occasions.

FRANCIS GOUHOUT

Confectioner.
(Corner of Main and Turnpike streets)

TAKES great pleasure in announcing to the
citizens of Hopkinsville and vicinity that
at his extensive confectionary establishment
may be found, at all times, all kinds of confections, such as

Pickles,	Venella Cream Candy,
French Brandy,	Sugar Toys,
Port Wine	Crystalized Candy,
Cordials	Venella Boston Candy,
Lemon Syrup,	Taffy Candy,
Orgeat "	Cough "
Cough "	Sugar Almonds,
Rose "	Mint Drops,
Ginger "	Lemon "
Satsaparilla "	Stick Candy
Raisins,	Crimped "
Fresh Prunes,	Kiss "
Brazil Nuts,	Cakes, all varieties,
Almonds,	et cetera.

The Ladies are respectfully invited to call,
As he has all manner of nice things suited to
Their taste and fancy.
Weddings and other parties furnished on
short notice.

~ Advertised in <u>The Kentucky Rifle </u>newspaper,
Hopkinsville, Kentucky, 1853

Fireplace or Woodstove?

Wood cooking stoves were first marketed in the 1830s. By 1847, they were in full commercial production and considered the "first major revolution in cooking since the discovery of fire," although not everyone agreed that this major cooking revolution was a great invention. Though perhaps a bit jokingly, Harriet Beecher Stowe wrote in her <u>Household Papers and Stories</u>, "Would our Revolutionary fathers have gone barefooted and bleeding over snows to defend air-tight stoves and cooking-ranges? I trow not. It was the memory of the great open kitchen fire, with its back log and fore stick of cord-wood, its roaring hilarious voice of invitation, its dancing tongues of flame, that called to them through the snows of that dreadful winter to keep their courage, that made their hearts warm and bright with a thousand reflected memories."

Both hearth and woodstove cooking are done at The Homeplace.

To make a wood fire in an open fireplace, begin by removing the andirons, and taking up all the ashes of the preceding night, and sweeping the hearth very clean. It is well to wash the hearth every morning before the new fire is made. Then bring forward what ever chunk of hot coals are found remaining from the fire that was covered up the night before; leaving sufficient space to put on a large back-log, on top of which place another log some what smaller. Lay a large fore-stick across the andirons, and upon it, place the live coals and chunks for kindling; adding, if necessary, some chips or bits of small wood. Then pile on two or three other sticks (placing the smallest at the top), take the bellows, and blow the fire into a flame till the wood is well ignited. It you wish a very large fire, pile two logs on the back-log, which ought to be of great size; and lay a large middle stick between the back-log and the fore-stick. Put on plenty of live coals and kindling, and add three or four good sized sticks (always placing the smallest at top), and then blow the fire well. If you place the small sticks underneath, they will shortly burn in two, and fall apart; bringing the upper ones down with them, and causing confusion and trouble!

~ Miss Eliza Leslie, <u>Household Book</u>, 1840

Banking the fire…"place chunks and hot coals on back-log, and throw over them ashes by shovel-fulls, till you have buried them entirely. This will keep the fire in till morning, when you uncover it to kindle with…"

~ Miss Eliza Leslie, <u>Household Book</u>, 1840

Notes for Your Homeplace

❖ *Mother is busy hoeing ground, preparing to plant peas today.*

> ~ February 28, 1860, Diary of Jane M. Jones

❖ *Made cold frame.*

> ~ March, 1859, Diary of Samuel Stacker

SPRING

❖ *Been day for good many jobs. Have meat peppered.*
Garden some. Mr G made me chicken coop - and some
frames for my rosebushes - set some hens - heard
yesterday the death of Aunt Hale.

> ~ Diary of Betty Gleaves, March 27, 1858

❖ *A hard freeze. All the fruit killed. Again I see it is the*
hand of God and I dare not murmur.

> ~ Diary of Jane M. Jones, April 6, 1857

❖ *Planted peach trees, picked rocks from orchard, flood*
took away cart.

> ~ Diary of Samuel Stacker, March, 1859

As now, spring for The Homeplace family was a time of renewal, welcomed with gathering wild greens, planting potatoes on Good Friday, and celebrating Easter by attending church services. Livestock was giving birth to their young. Hens were brooding to hatch out new chicks. Early spring floods renewed the soil, naturally fertilizing the fields.

Early spring crops of green peas, turnips and greens, carrots, cabbage, lettuce, radishes, onions, red beets were harvested from gardens. Garden seeds were saved from one year to the next, but seeds could also be purchased at the local general store. Shakers (in the area) were selling garden seeds in the 1850s with such popular varieties as long blood beets, yellow turnep, root radish, white silver skin onion, and ice head lettuce.

The gardens for anticipated summer and crop fields were plowed and planted with prayers for a large harvest. Many miles a day were walked behind the plow by the farm family. The entire family worked together to plant Indian corn and other cash crops. A large variety of vegetables were planted for the summer garden: early bunch cucumbers, Mexican and large red tomatoes, early sugar corn, early Valentine bunch, white vine or Dutch runner beans.

Join our Homeplace family in welcoming spring that will no doubt bring both sadness and joy.

❖ *Plant some seeds before breakfast.*

~ April 27, 1859, Diary of Betty Gleaves

J. J. Lampton

Fresh Seeds

A LARGE supply of Grass and Herd's Grass Seed; also a very general assortment of South Union Garden Seeds just received by

J J Lampton, Feb 24

~ The Kentucky Rifle newspaper, Hopkinsville, Kentucky
May 12, 1853

The Shakers were a religious group that lived in communities and among other industries, produced garden seeds. There were a number of Shaker Communities in the 1850s, including Pleasant Hill and South Union in Kentucky.

The quality seeds sold by the Shaker Community in Kentucky would have been available to The Homeplace farm.

W. Williams letter to his brother "…1 Book on Farming to be had at the seed store I forgit the name a small lott of garden seeds say Cabbage Beet parsnip onion early Bunch bean and any other kind of seeds that you may think a farmer may want to take a start from. I want the seed of a veary large Turnip for stock If to be had I want to so largely of them. A good quantity of cornfield Beans & Peas…"

A letter from Dover, Tennessee, nineteenth century

Garden Seeds Sold by the Shakers
at South Union, Kentucky, 1850:

Cabbage Large Drumhead

Cabbage Early-York

Cabbage Large Early

Cabbage Flat Dutch

Cabbage Curl Savoy

Beet Long Blood

Beet Early Red Turnep

Beet Early Sugar

Parsnep Long White

Radish Long Scarlet

Radish Crimson Turnep

Radish Yellow Turnep

Onion Large Red

Onion Large White

Turnep White Flat

Winter Turnep

Curl Mustard

Black Mustard

Cucumber Early Bunch

Squash Early Bunch

Pea Extra Early

Pea Early May

Bean Early Valentine

Bean White Vine

Orange Carrot

Lettuce Icehead

Lettuce White Loaf

Tomato Large Red

Celery White Solid

Parsley Double

Corn Early Sugar

Spinach Prickly Seeded

Pepper Grass

Improved Method of Making Coffee

Put your coffee (after grinding) into a flannel bag, tie it closely, allowing sufficient room to boil freely; put it into the boiler, adding as much water as may be required. After boiling, it will be perfectly clear, without the addition of eggs, &c., having likewise the advantage of retaining its original flavor and strength in greater perfection than when clarified.

~ Phineas Thornton, The Southern Gardener and Receipt Book, 1845

Without filtering methods, coffee grounds were separated from the liquid by many methods including adding whole raw eggs, egg shells, and cold water.

If flies come into the house, it is going to rain. If it rains before eleven, it will end before seven.

~ Farm folklore

Telling and Gathering Traditional Wild Foods

Information on gathering wild foods is included only for historical interest. We offer these recipes as a sample of historical methods of preparation, not as an encouragement of use.

Wild spring edible plants and early garden vegetables planted in the late winter provide a change from the monotonous diet of dried vegetables. Wild plants were collected while they were still young and tender. They not only provided food, they also provided natural dyes, much-needed medicines, and spring tonics that would thin the blood and keep you healthy through the summer months.

Washing Salads: To free salads from insects and worms, they should first be placed in salt water for a few minutes, to kill and bring out the worms, and then washed with fresh water in the usual way. This is an invaluable suggestion, as all salads are subject to insects, and some of them inconceivably small.

~ Phineas Thornton, The Southern Gardner and Receipt Book, 1845

Sassafras Tea

In the spring of the year,

When the blood is too thick,

There is nothing so fine

As a sassafras stick.

It tones up the liver,

And strengthens the heart,

And to the whole system

New life doth impart.

~ Southern saying, brought from Britain

Sassafras Tea

The sassafras roots need to be dug up in February. Once the roots are dug they must be washed thoroughly to remove all the dirt on the roots. Put a handful of preferably young roots into a pot with cold water and boil them until the rich red color comes to the water. Sweeten to taste with honey, maple syrup, or sugar. Drink up to your health.

~ The Homeplace Historical Recipe ~

Drink sassafras tea during the month of March and you won't need a doctor all year.

~ Folklore

Spring Beauty

Spring Beauty has long been a favorite of wild food enthusiasts. The small corms, or small bulb-like structures, closely resemble a miniature baked potato, but with a distinctive nutty flavor. This is the reason for one of the common names given this plant, fairy spuds.

~ Laura C. Martin, <u>Southern Wildflowers</u>

Because this is a beautiful spring flower, use ONLY where very abundant. In spring, pick leaves and dig tubers when identifiable by blossoms. Keep only the large tubers; replant others. Wash young leaves and nibble as a snack or chop a few in green salads. Wash tubers to remove all the dirt. Boil in water with a little salt about 10-15 minutes. Peel and serve whole, mashed, fried, or in salad.

~ The Homeplace Historical Recipe ~

Fiddleheads

Fiddleheads, so named because they look like the coiled tip of a fiddle's head, are the coiled tips of the fronds of young ferns.

Fiddleheads require careful cleaning of the scales or hairs, and cooking. Collect coiled fiddleheads up to eight inches in April, about the same time as flowering of Serviceberry trees in Middle Tennessee. Scrape inedible brown scales or hairs off by hand and wash in cold water. Once cleaned, steam to tenderness, they are delicious hot or cold. Ostrich fern and cinnamon fern fiddleheads should be steamed only as long as it takes to tenderize them, about ten minutes. Add seasoning and butter while hot.

~ The Homeplace Historical Recipe ~

Spicebush Tea

Spicebush tea was another common spring tonic. Spicebush is gathered in March when the bark slips. Gather a bundle of spice bush twigs, cover with four cups water, boil till the water changes color (fifteen to twenty minutes), strain through cheese-cloth, sweeten with honey, molasses, or sugar if you have, and enjoy.

~ The Homeplace Historical Recipe ~

Morels/Sponge Mushrooms

Morels are gathered throughout the United States at different times according to when spring comes to that area. Here in Middle Tennessee, folks who know mushrooms start looking for them from late March through early May. The best month is April. Morels are sometime called the Christmas tree mushroom because the caps are shaped like Christmas trees. After collecting the mushrooms, cut off soiled area and then soak what you are going to cook for the meal in salt water for several hours. Pour off the salt water and wash again. Combine cornmeal and salt and pepper to taste. Dip morels in cornmeal and deep fry in hot lard until golden brown.

~ The Homeplace Historical Recipe ~

Poke Weed / Poke Sallat

The Homeplace family would have known that while young poke is nutritious, pokeweed root is poisonous to people as are the purple black autumn berries. Mature stalks that turn purple are also toxic.

Gather young shoots up to six inches long in late spring before the leaves unfold. If the shoots show any purple coloration, they should be avoided. Older plants may be used if only the young tender leaves from the center of the very top of the plant are plucked.

To have enough to have a good mess, collect a large quantity of leaves, as cooking will greatly reduce the volume. Bring to boil and cook ten minutes. Change water and repeat. Change the water again. Then simmer slowly in a little salt water until water has almost cooked off, about thirty minutes. Add bacon drippings and fry about five minutes. If desired and to improve the flavor, add two to three eggs, slightly beaten, to poke sallat and cook until the eggs are done. Some folks like to put a little apple cider vinegar on their poke sallat. Enjoy.

~ The Homeplace Historical Recipe ~

When frogs croak, gather poke.

~ Southern folklore

Poke Asparagus

Poke, when gathered at the proper season and nicely dressed,
is considered by many people to be as fine as asparagus.
It is called poke asparagus,
and as such frequently cultivated in gardens:
it is the young tender stalks of the common pokeberry plant
that shoots forth in spring, and should be gathered
when about the size of asparagus of the largest size.
Scrape and cut the stalks of equal length,
soak them in fresh water
for an hour or two, and then boil them as directed for asparagus.
Serve them warm, lay round them on the edge of the dish
small buttered toasts,
and send them with a boat of melted butter,
seasoned with pepper.

~ Lettice Bryan, The Kentucky Housewife, 1839

Watercress

Collect young growth in fresh water spring nearly all year. Be sure to wash watercress several times to expel any water impurities and bugs. As a pot herb, cook and serve just like spinach or add to more bland fresh grated gingerroot. Watercress is an excellent soup ingredient. It is also great just raw and used raw as a garnish on sandwiches. The later in the season you gather watercress the spicier it may become.

~ The Homeplace Historical Recipe ~

Dandelions

The name dandelion dates back to medieval France. Due to the jagged edges of the plant leaves, the French called "dent-de-lion," meaning "tooth of the lion."

The dandelion was one of the more than 2000 herbs that were used when settlers came to North America. The roots have been used in tonics and liver cures, as well as to stop infections, skin diseases, dropsy, and to settle the digestive tract.

Dandelion Fritter

Pick blossoms developing or opened flower in the spring. Wash blossoms and set aside.

Combine a fritter batter, dip the blossoms in batter, and then fry in hot lard. Serve fritter with maple syrup, honey, or molasses.

~ The Homeplace Historical Recipe ~

Dandelion Greens

To eat dandelion greens pick the young green in early spring (late winter) before the blooms appear. Wash the young and tender greens well; place in a kettle, pour boiling water over them, let boil five minutes, drain, and season with salt and/or bacon fat. Young greens are also eaten raw with a little vinegar if you like.

~ The Homeplace Historical Recipe ~

Blow all of the seeds from a dandelion puffball
and your wish will come true.

~ Southern folklore

Gathering Early Spring Vegetables

"Why, they're just weeds!" That's how most twentieth century visitors react when they find the cook at The Homeplace preparing a mess of wild greens for the table. While again we caution that wild food information is for historical interest, you can try a mess of domestic garden greens from market or your own garden!

Cooked Garden Greens

Makes about six servings

3 pounds greens (any combination of turnip, mustard,
   or collard greens)
1 1/2 cups water
1/2 teaspoon salt
Freshly ground black pepper
1 piece of smoked hog jowl about 4 inches long and
   1 1/2 inches thick, or substitute 4 slices thick-cut bacon

Wash the greens several times under running water. Strip the green, fleshy part of the leaves from the stem and tear into small pieces. Discard the stems and all bruised or discolored leaves.

Slit the piece of hog jowl along the length at one inch intervals, cutting to but not through the rind. Put the hog jowl, the greens, and the water in a four to six quart kettle, and bring it to a boil. Stir, lower the heat, and simmer, covered for about forty-five minutes. Drain off the cooking liquid and reserve it for soup, or bring it to the table as a sauce for cornbread. Remove and discard the hog jowl from the greens. Add the salt and pepper to taste, and serve at once.

~ The Homeplace Recipe ~

Flower cookery, including using scented geraniums, roses, violets, and nasturtiums were a part of cooking in the 1800s.

Deep Fried Squash Blossoms

Makes four servings

8 squash blossoms
1/2 cup all-purpose
    flour
1/2 cup cornmeal
1/2 teaspoon salt
1 - 1 1/4 cups water
Lard for deep frying

Stir together the flour, cornmeal and salt in a deep bowl and pour in 1 cup of the water. Stir lightly to form a thin batter. If the batter appears too thick, you may add up to 1/4 cup more water. Set aside to chill in the refrigerator for about a half an hour.

Wash the squash blossoms and pat them completely dry. In a deep fat fryer or heavy skillet, melt the lard to the depth of three inches, and heat it until it is very hot (375°). Dip the squash blossoms in the batter and fry them in the hot fat for three to four minutes, or until they are golden and crisp. Drain. Serve immediately.

~ The Homeplace Recipe ~

❖ *Work some among my flowers--*
plant tomatoes and pepper seeds.
Cut some squares for Lizzy May's
hexagon quilt.

~ March 16, 1858,
Diary of Betty Gleaves

❖ *Spend morning working in garden - cut some Irish potatoes to plant. In evening, Mr. Gleaves plowed it up. Plant onions-peas-beats-radishes – burn off strawberry bed – plant some seeds.*

~ March 15, 1858, Diary of Betty Gleaves

Raw cabbage simply dressed with vinegar was "cold slaugh" to cookbook author Lettice Bryan in 1839; "hot slaugh" was cabbage fried in butter with the same seasoning.

Cabbage Salad

Makes eight servings

1 medium head of cabbage (about 1 ½ pounds)
1/3 cup cider vinegar
2 tablespoons brown sugar
1/2 teaspoon salt

Remove the tough outer leaves of the cabbage and cut the cabbage into quarters. Cut out and discard the core and slice the quarters crosswise into eighteen-inch-wide strips.

Combine the vinegar, the brown sugar, and the salt. Pour over the shredded cabbage and toss together gently. Serve at once.

~ The Homeplace Recipe ~

❖ *Set out more cabbage plants.*

~ April 23, 1856, Diary of Jane M. Jones

Turnips were a favorite at The Homeplace in 1850. Then and today, turnips offer edible greens just a few weeks after planting and peppery roots that can be stored where they grow.

Mashed Turnips and Potatoes

Makes eight servings

4 medium potatoes
  (about 2 pounds)
4 medium turnips
  (about 1 1/2 pounds)
4 quarts water
1 teaspoon salt

1/4 cup plus
  1 tablespoon butter,
  softened
1/4-1/2 cup heavy cream
1 teaspoon freshly
  ground black pepper

Wash the potatoes, peel them, and cut them into halves and quarters. Wash the turnips, peel them, and cut them into one-inch cubes. Put the potatoes and turnips in a three and one-half to four quart saucepan. Add the water and salt. Bring to a boil over high heat, then lower the heat, cover the pan, and simmer for about ten minutes, or until the turnips and potatoes are flaky and very soft. Drain in a colander, then return the vegetables to the pan in which they were boiled, shaking them over the heat for a few seconds until they are perfectly dry.

Mash with a wooden "beetle" or potato masher. Stir in the one-fourth cup butter a tablespoon at a time. Warm the cream slightly, then add about one half of it to the mixture, a tablespoon at a time. Then whip the potatoes and turnips with a slotted spoon or a fork, adding more cream as needed until the desired consistency has been reached. Stir in the pepper.

Spoon the mixture carefully into a heating serving dish. Make an indentation in the center with the back of a serving spoon and put in the remaining one tablespoon of butter. Serve immediately.

~ The Homeplace Recipe ~

Which Came First: The Chicken or Egg?

❖ *Got 168 chickens looking very nice.*
        ~ April 12, 1859, Diary of Betty Gleaves

❖ *Have chicken pie for dinner.*
        ~ May 23, 1859, Diary of Betty Gleaves

Chickens were very important for the farm family for food and income. Women and children took over the management of the chicken flock. Pens had to be kept clean, eggs collected daily, and predators had to be kept from killing the flock. In the spring, hens became 'broody' meaning they were ready to sit on a nest and hatch out chicks. The expansion of the flock was important for meat and eggs. Eggs were sold to local general stores and the women saved their egg money that paid for everyday needs for the farm family.

Preservation of Eggs

Relative to the preservation of eggs by immersion in lime-water, Mr. Preschier has given most satisfactory evidence of the efficacy of the process. Eggs, which he had preserved for six years in this way, being boiled and tried, were found perfectly fresh and good; and a confectioner of Geneva has used a whole cask preserved by the same means. In a small way eggs may be thus preserved in jars, or other vessels. They are to be introduced when quite fresh, the jar filled after the eggs are put in with lime-water, a little powdered lime sprinkled in at last, and then the jar closely corked. To prepare the lime-water, twenty or thirty pints of water are to be mixed with five or six pounds of slacked quick lime put into a covered vessel, allowed to clear by standing, and the lime-water immediately used.

~ Phineas Thornton, The Southern Gardener and Receipt Book, 1845

To Smother Young Chickens

Take two half grown chickens, split them open on the backs,
season them with salt, pepper, nutmeg, and lemon,
dredge them with flour, put them in a pan,
with four ounces of butter,
and enough water to cover them;
cover the pan and stew them slowly till they are very tender;
then add a handful of chopped parsley,
four boiled eggs, minced,
and a glass of port wine.
Serve up the chickens with the gravy poured round.

~ Lettice Bryan, The Kentucky Housewife, 1839

Sweet May has Come Again

Old winter's icy spell is o'er
The ides of March have flow....
The dusky clouds that darkened day,
And deepened sombre night,
The spring-time, now, has borne away,
And quenched in golden light,
And clothed is every hill and vale,
And blossomed ev'ry plain.
And perfumed now is ev'ry gale!
"Sweet May has come again."

So may the heart when winter reigns.
And grief and sorrow burn,
Find recompense for all its pains
When smiles of peace return;
"For thus do changing seasons show
That dearest hopes may wane,
But still the trusting heart may know,
That "May will come again."

May 4th, 1853   PRATHER

~ May 12, 1853, <u>The Kentucky Rifle</u>, Hopkinsville, Kentucky

Bees, Frolics and Pickin' Parties

In the winter, country roads and the rivers were nearly impassable; cabin fever was a real thing. By the spring, travel by country roads and rivers are much easier, to allow visiting and other entertainments. With the large amount of work on a farm, families would invite their friends and neighbors to help with the work. Work Bees and frolics were popular forms of entertainments. Music was always a part of any entertainment, and neighbors would get together for a Pickin' Party. The area between the rivers has a rich music tradition that goes back to their Celtic Roots. Old time fiddle tunes were handed down from father to son for generations. The Tennessee music box (dulcimer) is also part of that music tradition. Like today, songs reflected their lives, their loves and lost loves, memories of home and friends long passed, good times and bad. The importance of food to these rural people is heard in their songs.

The Homeplace Pickin' Party

Nineteenth Century period songs

Apple cider, un percimmon beer,

Christmas comes but once a year,

Ginger puddin and pumkin pie,

Gray cat kick dat black cat's eye

Oh, Jenny get de hoe cake done my dear,

Oh, Jenny get de hoe cake done, love!

~ Joel Walker Sweeney, 1840,
"Jenny Get Your Hoe Cake Done"

I'm a-going to eat at the welcome table,

I'm a-going to eat at the welcome table,

Some of these days.

I'm a-going to feast on milk and honey,

I'm a-going to feast on milk and honey,

Some of these days.

~ African American spiritual

Most music historians believe that the American banjo was based on African instruments made of hollowed gourds and animal skins. The ability to make these instruments was likely brought to America by black slaves who then made handcrafted instruments from long-necked, hollowed calabash gourds whose bowls were covered with a tight skin from coonskin or animal bladder. Eventually wooden banjos were made. It is likely that homemade banjos would have been favorites at The Homeplace, but the first commercially made banjos were made in the 1850s.

To Make a Bread Pudding

Take the crumbs of a small loaf of bread, and as much flour, the yolks of four eggs and two whites, a teaspoonful of ginger, half a pound of raisins seeded, half a pound of currants clean washed and picked, and a little salt; mix first the bread and flour, ginger, salt, and sugar to your taste, then the eggs and as much milk as will make it like a good batter; butter the dish, pour it in and bake it.

~ Phineas Thornton, <u>The Southern Gardener and Receipt Book</u>, 1845

Quilting Bees

Food was a big part of any social gathering. Quilts pieced during the winter months were ready to quilt when the weather was warm enough to put the quilt frame on the porch. Women would bring their best cakes, cookies and other treats to share with fellow quilters. In the evening the men would join the women for a play party with music, food and drink.

Almond Pound Cake

Beat to a cream one pound of butter
and one pound of powdered loaf sugar;
add two glasses of white wine,
a teaspoonful of powdered mace,
and the juice and grated rind of a lemon.
Blanch and pound to a paste
with a little rose water,
one pound of shelled sweet almonds:
sift a pound of flour,
beat to a froth twelve fresh eggs,
and stir the almonds, flour, and eggs alternately into the butter
&c.,
giving it a hard stirring at the last.
Put it into a deep pan of circular form, that is well buttered,
and bake it in a moderate oven.
When cold, ice it neatly with almond icing.

~ Lettice Bryan, The Kentucky Housewife, 1839

Almond Icing

Beat the whites of eggs to a stiff froth,
flavor it with a little oil of lemon,
and stir into it alternately
till quite thick and smooth,
equal portions of powdered loaf sugar and sweet almonds,
that have been pounded to a smooth paste,
and moistened with rose water as they were pounding,
to make them white and light.
Put it on the cakes as directed by other icing,
only put it on some thicker.

~ Lettice Bryan, The Kentucky Housewife, 1839

Basic Cake

1 1/4 cup flour
1 cup sugar
3/4 teaspoon cream of tartar
1/4 teaspoon baking soda
1/2 teaspoon salt
3/4 cup milk
1/3 cup soft, butter
1 egg, slightly beaten
1 tablespoon vanilla

Prepare pan. Beat all ingredients till smooth. Bake 30 minutes in moderate oven, 350 degrees. Cool 10 minutes, turn onto plate. Serve plain or top with well-cooked apples, or any other fruit or caramel sauce.

~ The Homeplace Recipe ~

Caramel Sauce
(Brown Sugar Sauce)

2 cups sugar
1 cup and 2 tablespoons milk
2 teaspoons butter
1 teaspoon vanilla

Using two skillets or saucepans. In one, put 1/2 cup of sugar, heat slowly until melts and turns brown. At the same time in the other skillet, combine the milk and 1 1/2 cups of sugar, heat to simmer. When sugar has browned in skillet one and milk-sugar mixture is at simmer, pour the browned sugar into the milk-sugar mixture. Continue cooking until the mixture comes to a soft ball stage. (Test by dropping it into a bowl of cold water, when cooled it should form a soft ball). When it is a soft ball stage, take off the heat and stir in butter and vanilla. Cool in bowl; cover the cake or use as a sauce for everyone to pour on their own piece of cake.

~ The Homeplace Recipe ~

In 1850, household guides instructed women to whip egg whites with hickory rods, the bare bones of a turkey wing, or the outstretched fingers of the hand.

1, 2, 3, 4 Cake is a recipe that is easy to remember just as the girls in the past had to remember recipes from their mother.

Cup Cake is as good as a pound cake, and is cheaper.

1, 2, 3, 4 Cake
(Cup Cake)

1 cup butter
2 cups sugar
3 cups of flour
4 eggs

Add 1 teaspoon of vanilla or historic flavorings below.

"One cup of butter, two cups of sugar, three cups of flour and four beaten eggs, a spoonful of cinnamon and a few spoonfuls of rose or lemon brandy. Commingle it very well, and bake it in small buttered pans with moderate heat."

~ Lettice Bryan, The Kentucky Housewife,1839

This Orange Pound Cake recipe was verbally given to The Homeplace farmwoman by a visitor; it was her family recipe that was at least 150 to 200 years old.

Orange Pound Cake

1 grated orange rind
2 cups sugar
3 cups plain flour
1 cup butter
1 1/4 cup buttermilk
1/2 teaspoon baking soda
1/2 teaspoon salt
4 eggs

Mix sugar and butter together, add eggs and grated orange; mix until creamy. Add soda, salt, flour and buttermilk. Bake in moderate oven at 350 degrees for 1 to 1 1/2 hours. Test with toothpick or broom straw; stick it in the center of cake, if it comes out clean it is done.

Frosting

Combine in saucepan or small iron skillet: 2 cups sugar to 1 cup orange juice and orange rind. Cook until softball stage, cool and pour over cake.

Rose water was distilled from rose petals and was used to flavor cakes before vanilla was popular. Vanilla and other extracts used to flavor cakes, like lemon brandy, was made by covering seasonal fruit peels from lemons and oranges with brandy or any other alcohol. The alcohol preserved the peel and the flavoring would leach into the alcohol, using a teaspoon or so to flavor a special cake.

Tea Cake

1 stick butter, softened
1 cup sugar
1 egg
1 teaspoon baking powder
1 teaspoon vanilla
2 cups flour
1/2 cup whole milk

Combine butter and sugar, and beat until fluffy. Add egg, vanilla, and baking powder and beat until well blended. Beat in flour, and then milk until the mixture is smooth. Butter a baking sheet and space evenly 6 heaping tablespoons of batter. Spread out each portion of dough into a circle the diameter of your hand. Top with sugar or colored sprinkles. Bake at 350 degrees fifteen minutes or until lightly browned.

~ Based on a nineteenth-century receipt

To hear a rain crow (a cuckoo) means rain.

~ Farm folklore

Kitchen Furnishings

Crockery. Brown earthen pans are said to be best, for milk and for cooking. Tin pans are lighter, and more convenient, but are too cold for many purposes. Tall earthen jars with covers, are good to hold butter, salt, lard, &c. The red earthen ware should never have acids put into it, as there are poisonous ingredients in the glazing, which the acid takes off. Stone ware is better and stronger and safer, every way, than any other kind.

Iron ware. Many kitchens are very imperfectly supplied with the requisite conveniences for cooking; and when a person has sufficient means, the following articles are all desirable. A nest of iron pots, of different sizes, (they should be slowly heated, when new); a long iron fork, to take out articles from boiling water; and iron hook, with a handle, to lift pots from the crane; a large and small gridiron, with grooved bars, and a trench to catch the grease; a Dutch oven, called, also, a bakepan; two skillets, of different sizes, and a spider, or flat skillet for frying; a griddle, a waffle-iron, tin and iron bake and bread-pans; two ladles, of different sizes; a skimmer; iron skewers; a toasting iron; two teakettles, one small and one large one; two brass kettles, of different sizes, for soap-boiling, &c. Iron kettles, lined with porcelain, are better for preserves. The German are the best. Too hot a fire will crack them, but with care in this respect, they will last for many years.

Portable furnaces, of iron or clay, are very useful, in summer, in washing, ironing, and stewing, or making preserves. If used in the house, a strong draught must be made to prevent the deleterious effects of the charcoal. A spice-box, spice, pepper, and coffee-mill, are needful to those who use such articles. Strong knives and forks, a sharp carving-knife, and iron cleaver and board, a fine saw, steel-yards, chopping-tray and knife, an apple-parer, steel for sharpening knives, sugar-nippers, a dozen iron spoons, also a large iron one with a long hand, six or eight flatirons, one of them very small, two iron-stand, a ruffle-iron, a crimping iron.

Tin Ware. Bread and cake-pans, a colander, and egg-boiler, a dredging-box, a large and small grater, large and small pattypans, cake-pans, with a centre tube to insure their baking well, pie-dishes, of block-tin, a covered butter-kettle, covered kettles to hold berries, two sauce-pans, a tin oven or tin kitchen, a tin apple-corer, and apple-roaster, a large oil-can with a cock, a lamp-filler, a tin lantern, broad-bottomed candlesticks for the kitchen, a candle-box, a funnel or tunnel, a tin reflector, for baking warm cakes, two sugar-scoops, and flour and meal-scoop, a set of tin mugs, three tin dippers, a pint, quart, and gallon measure, a set of scales and weights, three or four tin pails, painted on the outside, a tin slop-bucket, with a tight cover, painted on the outside, a milk-strainer, a gravy-strainer, a tin box, in which to keep cheese, also a large one for cake, and a still larger one for bread, with tight covers. Bread, cake, and cheese, shut up in this way, will not grow dry as in open air.

Wooden Ware. A nest of tubs, a set of pails, wooden-bowls, a large and small sieve, a beetle for mashing potatoes, a spad or stick for stirring butter and sugar, a bread-board, for moulding bread and making piecrust, a coffee-stick, a clothes-stick, a mush-stick, a meat-beetle, to pound tough meat, an egg-beater, a wooden ladle for working butter, a bread-trough (for a large family), flour buckets, with lids to hold sifted flour and Indian meal, salt-boxes, sugar-boxes, starch and indigo-boxes, spice-boxes, a bosom-board, a skirt-board, two or three clothes-frames and six dozen clothes-pins.

Basket Ware. Baskets, of all sizes, for eggs, fruit, marketing, clothes, &c., also chip-baskets. When often used, they should be washed in hot suds.

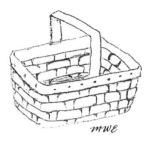

Other Articles. Every kitchen needs a box containing a ball of brown thread, a ball of twine, a large and small darning needle, a roll of waste-paper, a roll of old linen and cotton, and a supply of common holders….Also, two pudding or dumpling cloths, of thick linen, a gelly-bag, made of white flannel to strain gelly, a starch-strainer, and a bag for boiling clothes….

~ Catharine Beecher, <u>Treatise on Domestic Economy for the Use of Young Ladies at Home and at School</u>, 1841

Notes for Your Homeplace

❖ *Read my bible lesson in Job. Take a walk up on bluffs - gather some geological specimens.*

  ~ Sunday, May 22, 1859, Diary of Betty Gleaves

❖ *4 plough teams, 4 plough hands, planted potatoes.*

  ~ May 4, 1859, Diary of Samuel Stacker

SUMMER

❖ *A walk to the garden this evening is the first time I've been out - my babe has never caused me a moment's trouble. She sleeps all the while nearly & is so good.*

~ July 28, 1858, Diary of Betty Gleaves

❖ *I have not yet finished David's baptismal dress. Mr. Jones brought in some fine watermelons and peaches, so I have feasted. I love fruit <u>so dearly.</u>*

~ August 8, 1850, Diary of Jane M. Jones

❖ *We are all as merry as crickets.*

~ August 18, 1859, Diary of Jane M. Jones

Summer was a season of growing and of work on The Homeplace. Harvesting and planting would take place at the same time in the beginning of summer. Spring vegetables would be harvested. Some plants would be allowed to mature and seeds were saved for next years plants.

The houses were built with breezeways and separate kitchens to keep the houses cool. Especially in summer, most of the cooking was done in the morning hours. First thing of a morning, cook fires were lit in wood-fired cook stoves, or banked fires were revived in fireplaces, and breakfast preparation would begin. Breakfast was biscuits, grits, seasonal meat and gravy. The farm family would sit down to breakfast early in the morning.

 The women would pack leftover biscuits and meat for the menfolk as they left the house to go to the fields; the lunch would tide them over till dinner in the early afternoon. Women finished cooking dinner, then put on sunbonnets to join their children picking insects off garden plants, an early form of pest control.

The hard, hot work was done in the cooler hours of early morning and later in the evening. The work paused with the heat of the day, when the dinner bell was rung for the biggest meal of the day, dinner. Food provided at meals was seasonal. Less meat was eaten during the summer months, it was thought that too much meat in the summer would make you hot. Plus, salted pork was the only meat that could be preserved in the heat of the summer. Other meats, like chicken and fish were killed the same day it was eaten. Fresh fruits and vegetables were part of the meal. After dinner, the family rests or *noons* until the day cools a bit. Supper would have been leftovers from dinner or something as simple as a glass of buttermilk and cornbread.

By 1850, Donald L. Winters states in <u>Tennessee Farms, Tennessee Farming: Antebellum Agriculture in the Upper South,</u> the garden and orchard were major sources of food. Every household set aside a large plot near the house on which the family grew a wide variety of vegetables. The typical garden contained most of the following crops: several kinds of beans, Irish and sweet potatoes, peas, carrots, onions, beets, cabbage, squash, pumpkins, tomatoes, celery, turnips, parsnips, cucumbers, asparagus, melons, peppers, and radishes. Many farmers put out orchards that, after several years, provided apples, peaches, cherries, and plums; they sometimes planted strawberries and peanuts on the floor of orchards and grapes along the edge of the orchards or gardens.

Women and children's time would be devoted to the garden, picking off insects and weeds from vegetable plants to make sure the harvest was the best it could be.
~ 1840s diary of Keturah Penton Belknap

When the produce of the gardens and orchards was in season, family members ate fresh vegetables and fruits. But they always harvested ample amounts of preservable varieties to see them through the winter and early spring. They placed apples and root crops—potatoes, carrots, and turnips—in underground bins, cellars, or springhouses, where cool temperatures slowed their deterioration. They dried some fruits, such as peaches, apples, and plums, and kept them in closed containers. Glass jars with sealable lids became available for the first time, and some farm families canned vegetables and fruits. Because the jars were expensive and undependable—the loss from spoilage was high—

canning was not widely practiced. They pickled cucumbers, beets, and cabbage with homemade apple vinegar. They sweetened peaches, strawberries, cherries, and grapes with sugar, molasses, maple sugar or syrup, or honey to make jams and jellies. (Maple syrup was made in the area in the winter.) Apple cider and grape juice were popular beverages; blackberry wine and peach brandy provided stronger alternatives.

Photo by Denise Schmittou

All of this work in fields, garden, orchard, and home kept everyone busy. Even very young children helped to pick insects off vegetables, hoe fields and gardens for weed control, and harvest vegetables. But there was also time for fun! The Fourth of July was a major community celebration in the 1850s. The American Revolutionary War still in the collective memory was only a generation or two away from the people that lived in 1850. Ice Creams were made as a special treat for these celebrations.

By the dog days when the Dog Star was seen in the sky, fall plants were being planted, tradition has by the sixth of August. The dog days were also a time of illness and fevers.

In August and September, The Homeplace family might have packed food and traveled to a camp meeting where preachers would have preached long sermons, but friends would also have time to visit and eat meals together. Peddlers would have sold seasonal fruit, vegetables, gingerbread, and lemonade to supplement what had been brought from home - and young people might have a chance to court (meet potential mates).

Pull up a chair to the table or pack a basket for traveling and join us for summer at The Homeplace.

Summer Fare

Surrounded by rivers, fish was an abundant summer meat for farm families. Fresh chicken was also part of the summer fare. According to local farm families, every part of the chicken was eaten including their feet and head. Feet were boiled to loosen the skin around the tender meat underneath. Some say it was the best meat on the chicken. Heads were debeaked and decombed and fried with the neck and liver, heart, and gizzard.

In the 1850s, chickens were valued more for their eggs than for their potential as a dinner dish. Fried chicken was a semi-luxury item, saved for occasional Sunday dinners and special guests. An old story of the rural South, retold by historian Sam Bowers Hilliard, claimed the fowl were so "educated to the Sunday slaughter that when a 'genteel-looking' person approached the house, they fled to the woods."

Fried Chicken

Makes four servings

2 1/2 pound frying chicken, cut into serving pieces
1/2-1 cup lard
1 cup all-purpose flour
2 teaspoon salt
Freshly ground black pepper

Mix the flour with the salt and a few grindings of pepper. Wash the pieces of chicken under running water. Dry them thoroughly, and then dip each piece into the flour in the dish, turning to coat it evenly. Shake off the excess flour.

Melt the lard in a heavy skillet large enough to hold all the pieces of chicken at once. The melted lard should reach a depth of one-half inch.

Add the pieces of chicken to the skillet, beginning with the thighs and legs, and then adding the breasts and wings. Fry over medium-high heat for six to eight minutes on each side until browned. Cover the skillet and lower the heat. Continue to cook for thirty to forty minutes. To crisp the chicken, remove the cover of the skillet and cook for ten minutes more.

Remove the chicken from the skillet, drain, pile on a heated platter and serve immediately.

~ The Homeplace Recipe ~

Chicken Pie

Parboil and cut up neatly two young chickens. Take the water in which they have been boiled to make a gravy, put in pepper and salt, and a thickening of flour and butter. Make a puff paste crust, and cover your pan. Boil six eggs hard, and put the yolks, cut in two, into the pie, along with the chicken; a few oysters may be laid round among the chicken. Fill the pan with gravy and cover with a thick crust. It will require about an hour and a half to bake.

~ Phineas Thornton, <u>The Southern Gardener and Receipt Book,</u> 1845

Chicken Salad

Boil a chicken that does not exceed in weight a pound and a half. When quite tender, take it up, cut in small strips, and prepare the following sauce and pour on it. Boil four eggs three minutes; take them out of the shells; mash and mix them with two spoonfuls of drawn butter, twelve of vinegar, a teaspoon of mixed mustard the same of salt, a little pepper and essence of celery.

~ A.L. Webster, <u>The Improved Housewife,</u> 1858

The streams, creeks, and rivers near The Homeplace are alive with fish: channel, blue, and flathead catfish; smallmouth bass and Kentucky spotted bass; and various bream or sunfishes. Catfish, then and now, is a Southern favorite. Surrounded by rivers, fish was an abundant summer meal for farm families. As with chicken, nothing of the fish was wasted. According to local tradition, fish heads were cooked in stew, producing a very smelly kitchen.

❖ *Mr. Jones took the children fishing.*

~ July 2, 1856, Diary of Jane M. Jones

Fried Catfish

Makes 4 servings

3 pounds fresh catfish, cleaned and skinned
1 1/2 cups white, stoneground cornmeal
2 teaspoons salt
Freshly ground black pepper
Lard or bacon drippings for frying
Vinegar

Pour the cornmeal into a shallow pan and dip the pieces of fish in the meal to coat them thoroughly. Dust with salt and a few grindings of black pepper.

Melt the lard or the drippings in a heavy twelve-inch iron skillet to a depth of at least one/half inch. Heat the fat until it is very hot, then add the fish. Fry over medium heat until brown on one side, about five minutes, and then turn the fish carefully, and fry another five minutes, or until they are evenly browned. Remove the catfish to a warm platter and serve at once. Pass vinegar for seasoning or slices of onion.

~ The Homeplace Recipe ~

Cat-fish Soup

Cat-fish that have been caught near the middle of the river are much nicer than those that are taken near the shore where they have access to impure food. The small white ones are the best. Having cut off their heads, skin and clean and cut them into threes. To twelve small fish, allow a pound and a half of ham. Cut the ham into small pieces, or mouthfuls and scald it two or three times in boiling water, lest it be too salt. Chop together a bunch of parsley and some sweet marjoram stripped from the stalk. Put these ingredients into a soup kettle and season them with pepper; the ham will provide enough salt. Add a head of celery cut small, or a large tablespoonful of celery seed tied in muslin. Put in two quarts of water, cover the kettle, and let it boil slowly till everything is quite tender. Skim it frequently. In another pot, boil a quart of rich milk, in which you have melted a ¼ pound of butter divided into small bits and rolled in flour. Pour it hot into the soup, and stir in the beaten yolks of 4 eggs. Boil it enough to take out the rawness of the eggs and put it in a tureen, and add toasted bread cut into squares.

~ Eliza Leslie, <u>Directions for Cookery, in its Various Branches</u>, 1848

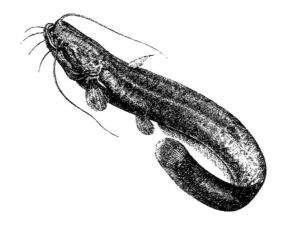

Fried Bacon or Jowl

Go to the smoke house and cut the amount of bacon or jowl meat you will need for the meal. Slice into smaller pieces and soak in warm water for at least a half hour to remove excess salt. After soaking, dip the meat in flour or cornmeal. Heat skillet, melt about a tablespoon of lard, enough to cover the bottom of a skillet. Add the breaded meat and fry until golden brown.

~ The Homeplace Recipe ~

How did red-eye gravy get its name? When the coffee and grease are combined, the mixture does look like a red eye. Tradition has it that when Andrew Jackson of Tennessee, served a portion of country ham and the rich, dark gravy by a cook who had obviously been tippling at the whiskey barrel, commented, "That gravy is as brown as the cook's red eyes!"

Country Ham and Red-eye Gravy

4 servings

4 slices country ham, cut 1/4 inch thick
1 cup strong cold coffee

Trim the excess fat from the slices of country ham. Rub the bottom of a heavy cast iron skillet with enough ham fat to grease it thoroughly, and then heat the skillet until it is very hot. Add the ham slices, and sear them on both sides, regulating the heat so that they brown evenly.

Pour the coffee into the skillet. Bring it to a boil, and then lower the heat and simmer gently for about ten minutes, or until the ham is tender. Most of the gravy will have evaporated, but there should be enough left to moisten the ham. Serve immediately, preferably with hot biscuits.

~ The Homeplace Recipe ~

To Boil a Ham

Smoked hams should be soaked in fresh water for twelve hours before they are boiled, and if very dry, twenty-four hours will still be better. Put the ham in a large pot of cold water, and boil it slowly till it is done, which will take hours, carefully removing the scum as it rises to the top. When it is sufficiently tender (which you may tell by trying it with a fork), draw off the skin carefully and smoothly, so as to preserve the skin whole, and not tear the ham, to make it look ragged. Trim it nicely, and spot it over at intervals with red pepper; wrap a bunch of curled parsley round the shank bone, which should be sawed short, and garnish with small bunches of asparagus, which have been neatly prepared and served upon buttered toasts. Accompany it with stewed fruit and green vegetables. After dinner skewer on the skin again, to prevent its getting dry.

~ Lettice Bryan, The Kentucky Housewife, 1839

A Ham Pie

Having a fine young fowl cleaned and cut up in the usual manner, season it with salt and pepper, and stew it till nearly done in a small quantity of water. Cut some thin small slices of boiled ham and season with pepper and mace. Roll out a thick crust of standing or dripping paste; line the bottom and sides of a deep dish with it; roll out another sheet of the paste, cut it into small squares, and fill the dish with the slices of ham, fowl and dumplings, put in alternately; then put in liquor in which the fowl was stewed, with four ounces of butter rolled in flour and broken up. Put a paste over the tip, ornament it round and edge with paste over the top, ornament it round the edge with scalloped or crimped leaves of the same, and bake it in a moderate oven; it will not require but a short time to bake.

~ Lettice Bryan, The Kentucky Housewife, 1839

Cucumbers Dressed Raw

They should be as fresh from the vine as possible, few vegetables being more unwholesome when long gathered. As soon as they are brought in, lay them in cold water. Just before they are to go to table, take them out pare them and slice them into a pan of fresh cold water. When they are sliced, transfer them to a deep dish, season them with a little salt and black pepper, and pour over them some of the best vinegar, to which you may add a little salad oil. You may mix with them a small quantity of sliced onions, not to be eaten, but to communicate a light flavor of onion to the vinegar.

~ Eliza Leslie, <u>Directions for Cookery, in its Various Branches</u>, 1848

Tomatoes, Squash, Okra, and Peas

Brought to the Americas from Africa, the word Okra comes from okura, the plant's name in the Igbo language of the African country, Nigeria.

Okra and Tomatoes

2 pounds okra, cleaned
1 medium onion, chopped
1/4 cup butter
4 medium tomatoes, peeled and coarsely chopped
1/2 teaspoon salt
1/4 teaspoon pepper

Cut okra crossways, and set aside. Sauté onion in butter in heavy skillet over medium heat, until tender. Add okra, tomatoes, salt and pepper, Stir well. Cook over medium heat for 30 minutes. Stirring frequently

~ Mary Randolph, <u>TheVirginia Housewife</u>, 1838

Stewed Tomatoes

Use 8 to 10 ripe tomatoes. Peel them and cut them in quarters. Put them into a skillet or kettle with a little water and add to them pepper and salt to taste, 1 to 2 tablespoon of brown sugar, 1 tablespoon of butter. Stew them slowly until cooked, add one or two crumbled day old biscuits. Cook slowly until dry.

~ The Homeplace Recipe ~

Stewed Okra

Pick okra in morning hours to preserve sweetness as with any vegetable. Wash, but don't cut off the stems or cut into the okra. Place the amount needed for a meal about one to two cups of washed okra in a kettle cover with water, add two to four tablespoons of vinegar or to taste and amount of okra, and a teaspoon of butter, salt and pepper to taste. Boil slowly until the okra is tender fifteen to twenty minutes. Eat the okra, but not the stems. The vinegar will keep the okra from becoming slimy, so some vinegar needs to be added.

~ The Homeplace Recipe ~

Green Peas

Green peas are unfit for eating when they become hard and yellowish; but they are better when nearly full grown than when very small and young. They should be gathered as short a time as possible before they are cooked, and laid in cold water as soon as they are shelled. They will require about an hour to boil soft. When quite done, drain them, mix with them a piece of butter, and add a little pepper.

*Peas may be greatly improved by boiling with them two or three lumps of loaf-sugar and a sprig of mint to be taken out before they are dished. This is an English way of cooking green peas and to most tastes a very good one.

~ Eliza Leslie, <u>Directions for Cookery, in its Various Branches</u>, 1848

Boiled Green Beans

These beans should be young, tender, and fresh gathered. Snap off both ends of the bean and remove the strings. Then break or cut them in two or three pieces. Put them in a kettle with fresh water and boil until very tender. Add a tablespoon or so of bacon grease or lard or add a piece of butter. Salt and pepper to taste. The juice remaining on the bottom of the kettle or pot liquor is delicious and was often absorbed by a piece of corn bread.

~ The Homeplace Recipe ~

Scarlet [Runner] Beans

It is not generally known that the pod of the scarlet bean, if green and young, is extremely nice when cut into three or four pieces and boiled. They will require nearly two hours, and must be drained well, and mixed as before mentioned with butter and pepper. If gathered at the proper time, when the seed is just perceptible, they are superior to any of the common beans.

~ Eliza Leslie, <u>Directions for Cookery, in its Various Branches</u>, 1848

Jonathan's Favorite Squash Fritters

2 cups grated yellow summer squash, drained
1/2 cup grated onion
6 tablespoons flour
1 egg
Salt and pepper to taste

Grate squash and onion and set aside in a colander to drain. Squeeze remaining water from squash and onions and mix with beaten egg, salt, pepper and flour. Heat greased skillet and drop the squash batter with a spoon. Cook until golden brown.

~ The Homeplace Recipe ~

Creamed Summer Squash

Makes about six servings

10 baby yellow crookneck
    squash, 4-5 inches in
    length
4 cups water
1/4 cup cream

1 tablespoon butter
1/4 teaspoon salt
Freshly ground black
    pepper

Wash the squash under running water, rubbing off the fuzz with your fingers. Cut off the stalk end, but do not cut into the flesh of the squash. Bring the water to a boil in a two and one/half to three quart saucepan. Add the whole squash, lower the heat, and simmer for about twenty-five minutes until the squash is very soft. Drain in a colander, discarding the water, and return the squash to the pot in which they were cooked. Then mash them with a wooden "beetle" or a potato masher. Add the cream and the butter and beat with a slotted spoon or a fork until all the ingredients are well combined and the squash is a creamy mass. Add the salt and a few grindings of black pepper. Spoon into a heated vegetable dish and serve at once.

~ The Homeplace Recipe ~

Cymblings

There is only one nice way of preparing
summer squash or cymblings.
Gather them when very young and soft,
so that you can nip the peeling or rind with your nail;
then they have their full flavor;
the seeds are nothing more than blisters,
and the whole of cymblings are good to eat;
do not cut them to pieces before they are boiled,
as, to boil them in clear water after they are cut up,
makes them insipid. Rinse them clean,
put them in a pot of boiling water, with a handful of salt,
and boil them gently till they are done very tender;
then drain and mash them fine,
pressing the pulp through a cullender,
put it in a sauce-pan, with a good lump of butter,
rolled in flour, some pepper, and a glass of rich sweet cream;
set it over a few coals, and stir it constantly
till it absorbs the seasonings, and becomes nearly dry.
It is usually served with roast meats.
There are various colors and sizes
of the summer squash, but all should be dressed alike,
except when they get very large, and rather old; of course
they should be split,
and the seeds taken out before they are boiled,
though at such an age they are not good.

~ Lettice Bryan, The Kentucky Housewife, 1839

The Fourth of July

❖ *In the evening went to a great circus, "Welch Delevan, & Mathaws" is said to be the best in the world. I think very fine but am no judge as it is the only I ever saw.*

~ July 4, 1850, Diary of Jane M. Jones

❖ *Ma calls on her way to sisters - very anxious for me to go with her, but I am not well enough. Feel very badly all day in a great deal of pain. I gave birth to a fine daughter at sun set.*

~ July 4, 1860, Diary of Jane M. Jones

The fourth of July was celebrated here with a degree of spirit, and in a style we have never before witnessed in Clarksville.... A public barbecue and speaking was announced which attracted crowds of people, males and females, from all parts of the country.

At daylight, the church bells rang out their merry peals, calling to mind the fact that the anniversary of our independence had again rolled around. About 9 o'clock the procession was formed upon the square. The fire companies and their engines and hose reels made their appearance, and by the beauty of their arrangements and the taste and elaborateness of their decorations excited the liveliest surprise and admiration. Each engine was covered with a splendid platform, from which rose a canopy, beautifully designed and sustaining innumerable flags, and ornamental work of beauty. On the platforms were seated several beautiful children, charmingly dressed who gave a delightful finish to the decorations. The companies, the Eagle numbering 61 men and the Deluge 40 men, in respective uniforms, preceded by the Brass Band in an immense car drawn by four horses, formed in procession, and after passing through the principal streets, reached the barbecue ground. A stand had been erected for speakers and seats provided for the ladies.

The Declaration of Independence was read in capital style by Dr. Cooper, and addresses were delivered by Thos. W. Wisdom, Esq., and by Rev. Mr. Baird and Rev. J.T. Hendrick, after which dinner was announced.

The most generous provision had been made for the stomachs of the crowd. The dinner was well prepared, ample as to quantity, and gave universal satisfaction.

~ Clarksville Jeffersonian,
July 11, 1855

The celebrations for the Fourth of July, The United States' Independence Day, were some of the most elaborate public celebrations of the nineteenth century. People flocked to nearby cities to experience parades, band concerts, and patriotic readings of the Declaration of Independence. And, of course, food was an important part of the celebration!

Lemonade and limeade, when available, were popular drinks. Strawberries were a treat. Public dinners might have included barbeque, ham and other meats, biscuits, pickles (a good time to show off the best), cakes and pies, but a favorite treat was ice cream.

The hand-cranked ice cream freezer had been patented and was being sold commercially by the late 1840s, making homemade ice cream easier to make, as shown by an ad that appeared in Godey's Lady's Book in 1850:

Ice cream has become one of the necessities of life. A party without it would be like breakfast without bread…

~ Godey's Lady's Book, August 1850

It is likely, though, that especially among farm families who watched expenses, the old-fashioned freezers, or even tin pails, would also have been still used. Ice and rock salt (sometimes called ice-cream salt) would have been necessary for the freezing.

Thick blocks of ice might still have been cut from frozen ponds in winter, but by the mid-1800s, commercial shipping of ice from north to south by steamboats and later by rail was common. Those who could afford ice houses would have had ice to keep and to sell. Ice would have likely been purchased from merchants by those at The Homeplace.

To Make Ice Cream

To make Ice Cream. One quart of milk. One and half tablespoon-fuls of arrowroot. The grated peel of two lemons. One quart of thick cream. Wet the arrowroot with a little cold milk and add it to the quart of milk when boiling hot; sweeten it very sweet with white sugar, put in the grated lemon peel, boil the whole, and strain it into the quart of cream. When partly frozen, add the juice of two lemons. Twice this quantity is enough for thirty-five persons. Find the quantity of sugar that suits you by measure, and then you can use this every time, without tasting. Some add whites of eggs, others think it is just as good without. It must be made very sweet, as it loses much by freezing.

If you have no apparatus for the purpose (which is almost indispensable), put the cream into a tin pail with a very tight cover, mix equal quantities of snow and brown salt (not the course salt) or of pounded ice and salt, in a tub, and put it as high as the pail, or freezer, turn the pail of freezer half round and back again with one good hand, for half an hour, or longer, if you want it very nice. Three quarters of an hour steadily, will make it good enough. While doing this, stop four or five times, and mix the frozen part with the rest, the last time very thoroughly, and then the lemon juice must be put in. Then cover the freezer tight with snow and salt till it is wanted. The mixture must be perfectly cool before being put in the freezer. Renew the snow and salt while shaking, so as to have it kept tight to the sides of the freezer. A hole in the tub holding the freezing mixture to let off the water, is a great advantage. In a tin pail it would take much longer to freeze than in the freezer, probably nearly twice as long, or one hour and a half. A long stick, like a coffee stick, should be used in scraping the ice from the side. Iron spoons will be affected by the lemon juice, and give it a bad taste.

In taking it out for use, first wipe off every particle of the freezing mixture dry, then with a knife loosen the sides, then invert the freezer upon the dish in which the ice is to be served, and apply two towels rung out of hot water to the bottom part, and the hole will slide out in the shape of a cylinder. If you wish to put it into moulds, pour it into them when the cream is frozen sufficiently, and then cover the moulds in snow and salt till they are wanted. Dip the moulds in warm water to make the ice slip out easily.

If you wish to have a freezer made, send the following directions to a tinner.

Make a tin cylinder box, eighteen inches high and eight inches in diameter at the bottom, and a trifle larger at the top, so that the frozen cream will slip out easier. Have a cover made with arm to lap over three inches, and fitted tight. Let there be a round handle fastened to the lid, an inch in diameter, and reaching nearly across, to take hold of, to stir the cream. This will cost from fifty to seventy-five cents.

The tub holding the ice and freezer should have a hole in the bottom, to let the water run off, and through the whole process the ice must be close packed the whole depth of the freezer.

Modern ice cream recipe using 6 cups sugar, 6 eggs, separated, 10 tablespoons flour, 2 quarts cream/milk, dash of salt, 6 tablespoons vanilla. Scald milk and add sugar, flour and salt. Mix well. Add beaten egg yolks. Cook until thickened. When cool, add beaten egg whites and vanilla. To freeze, add 3 pints whipping cream and the rest milk. Makes 3 gallons.

~ Catharine Beecher, Miss Beecher's Domestic Receipt Book, 1850

To Make Ices

If you do not have a freezer, the process may be very easily accomplished by putting the cream into a tin pail, and setting it into a pail or small tub filled with coarse salt and lumps of ice. When the cream begins to freeze around the edge, stir it thoroughly, and then shake the pail about until it is well frozen.

~ H. M. Cornelius, The Young Housekeeper's Friend, 1846

Strawberry or Raspberry Ice Cream

Bruise a pint of raspberries, or strawberries, with two large spoonfuls of fine sugar; add a quart of cream and strain through a sieve, and freeze it. If you have no cream, boil a spoonful of arrow-root in a quart of milk, and if you like, beat up one egg and stir into it.

~ H. M. Cornelius, The Young Housekeeper's Friend, 1846

Common Ice Cream

Split into pieces a vanilla bean, and boil it in a very little milk till the flavour is well extracted; then strain it. Mix together two table-spoonfuls of arrow-root powder, or the same quantity of fine powdered starch, with just sufficient cold milk to make it a thick paste; rubbing it till quite smooth. Mix together a pint of cream and a pint of rich milk; and afterwards stir in the preparation of arrow-root, and the milk in which the vanilla has been boiled. Beat it very hard, stir in half a pound of powdered loaf-sugar, beating it very hard again. Then strain it, and put it into a freezer placed in a tub that has a hole in the bottom to let out the water; and surround the freezer on all sides with ice broken finely, and mixed with coarse salt. Beat the cream hard for half an hour. Then let it rest; occasionally taking off the cover, and scraping down with a long spoon the cream that sticks to the sides. When it is well frozen, transfer it to a mould; surround it with fresh salt and ice, and then freeze it over again. If you wish to flavour it with lemon instead of vanilla, take a large lump of sugar before you powder it, and rub it on the outside of a large lemon till the yellow is all rubbed off upon the sugar. Then, when the sugar is all powdered, mix it with the juice.

For strawberry ice cream, mix with the powdered sugar the juice of a quart of ripe strawberries squeezed through a linen bag.

~ Eliza Leslie, Directions for Cookery, in its Various Branches, 1848

Independence Day Ice Cream

1 quart cream
1 quart good sweet milk
2 cups sugar
vanilla extract to taste

Put in churn and turn until froze. Scrape sides with spoon once it starts to freeze; helps to freeze faster.

~ The Homeplace Recipe ~

Making ice cream at The Homeplace

Our great national anniversary was celebrated here with out much system, or a great deal of display, though not without considerable excitement. Our business houses were closed, and everybody seemed to be looking for something to do. Not much, however, was accomplished to this line until after dinner, when various schemes of employment were perfected. One was a picnic at the Dunbar Cave, another was an excursion on the Railroad. Some two or three hundred took passage and seven large platform cars were crowded full. The excursionists went to the end of the road, and had a jolly time.

There was also a land sale, as it was called, at McClure's Spring, at which some twenty or thirty lots were knocked off cheap....

There was a good deal of getting drunk and getting mad over it, in various parts of town, resulting in innumerable fights of various sizes. One Irishman inserted his nose in his antagonist's mouth for the purpose of holding him, and thereby lost the end of the very important member.

Nothing in the shape of accident occurred anywhere to disturb the general hilarity.

~ Clarksville Jeffersonian,
July 9, 1856

❖ *I am making a blackberry cordial.*

~ July 3, 1856, Diary of Jane M. Jones

❖ *I am making more cordial. Jim Cook is dead got over heating and drank too much.*

~ July 4, 1856, Diary of Jane M. Jones

❖ *We all come up for a "Sons of Temperance" celebration at Middleburgh...Mr. Young from Memphis spoke.*

~ July 4, 1857, Diary of Jane M. Jones

A popular drink in the 1850s dating from Colonial times was shrub, a fruit-based drink. For those not in the Temperance Movement, brandy or rum was added. Though lemon was a favorite flavor in the 1800s, lemons had to be purchased, so other local raised fruits were used in shrubs. The best available thirst quenchers for a hot summer day were fruit shrubs or switzels, sweet to the taste but tart on the back of the throat. According to food author Laura Moorhead, "shrub is probably derived from the Arabic shurb, meaning 'drink.'"

Blackberry Shrub or Switzel

Makes about 1 1/2 quarts of syrup

2 pounds fresh blackberries
4 cups cider vinegar
4 cups sugar

Three days before you wish to make the shrub, put the blackberries in a glass or ceramic bowl, pour in the vinegar, cover, and set aside. Let the blackberries soak for three days in the vinegar at room temperature. Then pour the contents of the bowl into a fine mesh strainer and press down hard on the blackberry pulp to extract as much juice as possible. Pour the liquid into a two quart saucepan, add the sugar, and bring to a boil, stirring constantly until the sugar has dissolved. Boil the mixture for about two minutes, then remove from the heat and cool. To serve, add one-fourth cup blackberry syrup to one cup cold water in a tall glass.

~ The Homeplace Recipe ~

Fruit Switzels were drank by people that worked and sweated a lot to replenish their lost minerals.

Basic Recipe for Switzel

To 2 quarts of water, add:

1/4 cup vinegar
1 cup sugar and
1/2 teaspoon ginger

Add fruit syrup of choice.

~ The Homeplace Recipe ~

Indian Corn

When the oak leaves are the size of a mouse's ear, it is time to plant corn.

~ Farm folklore

White corn meal was a favorite of the South, but at The Homeplace the Indian corn that was raised came in many different colors. Almost all cornmeal breads can be made with any white, yellow or other colored meal, the finished product will vary slightly. White meal gives a pleasantly uneven texture, a crisper outside, and a softer inside. Breads made with yellow cornmeal are drier, more even-textured, and slightly granular.

The Homeplace Heirloom Corn Varieties

Hickory King

Bloody Butcher

Reid's Yellow

Virginia Gourdseed

Cherokee White Eagle

Cherokee Long Ear Popcorn

Stowell's Evergreen*

*This heirloom variety was introduced in 1848, one of the oldest white sweet corns that can be traced back to American Indians. This field corn stays "in milk" longer than any other field corn. "In milk" means that the corn can be eaten as corn on the cob, also known as green corn, hence, the name evergreen.

Known as Indian corn (cookbooks from this time often refer to Indian meal rather than corn meal), the corn that fed the family at The Homeplace also fed the stock and was an important cash crop. A food introduced to settlers to the New World by Native peoples, corn is actually maize. The term corn was used by the British to refer to any kind of grain. The Native Americans in The Homeplace area would have most likely been Cherokee and Chickasaw.

Spoonbread

Makes six servings

5 tablespoons butter
2 cups water
1 cup white, stoneground cornmeal
1 cup milk
1 teaspoon salt
4 eggs

Preheat the oven to 375°.

Melt the five tablespoons butter in a one quart baking dish placed in the preheated oven for about ten minutes. Bring the water to a boil in a one and one/half to two quart saucepan. Remove from the heat and add the cornmeal in a slow stream, stirring constantly. Continue to stir until the mixture is thick and smooth. Stir in the milk and the salt. Add the eggs, one at a time, beating hard after each addition. Stir in the melted butter, and pour the batter into the baking dish. Bake in the center of the oven for about 35 minutes, or until the top of the spoonbread is golden brown and firm in appearance.

Serve at once with plenty of soft butter.

~ The Homeplace Recipe ~

Batter cakes, or batty cakes, are thin pancakes made of cornmeal. At The Homeplace, batter cakes are topped with molasses whip: butter and molasses beaten together with a fork.

Batter Cakes
Fried Cornbread

Makes about two dozen cakes

1/2 cup white stoneground cornmeal
1/2 teaspoon salt
2/3 cup buttermilk
1 egg, lightly beaten
Bacon fat or butter for greasing skillet

Stir together the cornmeal and the salt in a small mixing bowl. In another bowl, beat together the egg and the buttermilk and pour it over the cornmeal mixture. Beat until the batter is very smooth.

Heat a heavy skillet over medium heat. With a pastry brush, grease it lightly with the bacon fat or butter.

Spoon about one tablespoon of batter into the skillet for each cake. Fry four to five cakes at once for two to three minutes, until the topside is bubbly and the underside is golden brown. Turn the cakes over, and fry for a few seconds to firm the other side. Remove to a warmed plate and keep covered until all cakes are fried. Serve at once. Pass butter, honey, jam, and molasses.

~ The Homeplace Recipe ~

"Perhaps no bread in the world is as good as Southern cornbread," wrote Mark Twain, and added, "perhaps no bread in the word is as bad as the Northern imitation of it."

Skillet Cornbread

Makes one nine-inch bread (6-8 servings)

3 tablespoons lard
1 1/2 cups white stoneground cornmeal
1/2 cup all-purpose flour
1 teaspoon baking soda
1/2 teaspoon salt
1 1/2 cups buttermilk
1 egg

Preheat oven to 400 degrees.

Heat the lard in a nine-inch iron skillet over moderate heat until the lard has melted. Set aside. Combine the cornmeal, flour, baking soda, and salt in a mixing bowl. In another bowl, beat the egg lightly with a fork, then stir in the buttermilk and the melted lard. Pour the buttermilk mixture over the cornmeal mixture and stir together just until the batter is smooth.

Pour the batter into the prepared skillet. Bake in the center of the oven for about twenty minutes or until the top of the bread is golden brown and the sides have begun to draw away from the edges of the skillet. Cut into wedge-shaped pieces and serve at once.

~ The Homeplace Recipe ~

> Green maize, which refers not to color but to young corn…was a tremendous favorite and in many tribes became the focus of specific ceremonies. These cobs were "in the milk," containing a milky liquid in their unripe kernels that could be scraped off cobs with mussel or oyster shells or half a deer's jaw before being pounded into liquid. This was the origin of creamed corn and green-corn pudding.
>
> ~ Linda Murray Berzok, <u>American Indian Food</u>

Green Corn Pudding

Makes about 6 servings

2 cups fresh corn kernels,
    or substitute 2 cups canned or frozen corn kernels
4 tablespoons all-purpose flour
2 eggs
2 cups milk
1 teaspoon salt
2 tablespoons butter

Preheat the oven to 350°.

With one tablespoon of butter, grease the bottom and sides of a two quart casserole dish. Set aside.

Stir together the flour, corn, and salt in a mixing bowl. In another bowl, beat the eggs lightly with a fork, and then stir in the milk and the remaining tbs. of butter, melted. Pour the liquid mixture over the corn and stir together.

Pour into the prepared pan and bake for fifty minutes. After ten minutes, stir the contents of the pan, combining the bottom layer of partially cooked batter with the still-liquid center. Stir a second time in ten more minutes. The pudding is done when a knife inserted in the center comes out clean. Serve at once, directly from the dish.

~ The Homeplace Recipe ~

Although sweet corn varieties were available to mid-nineteenth-century farmers, Homeplace families generally did not raise it in their gardens. They preferred to eat field corn that was still in the milk stage for corn on the cob or fried corn. Such corn is referred to as 'green corn' in period sources.

Indian Corn

Corn for boiling should be full grown but young and tender. When the grains become yellow it is too old. Strip it of the outside leaves and the silk, but let the inner leaves remain, as they will keep in the sweetness. Put it in a large pot with plenty of water, and boil it rather fast for half an hour. When done, drain off the water, and remove the leaves.

*You may either lay the ears on a large flat dish and send it to the table whole, or broken in half; or you may cut all the corn off the cob, and serve it up in a deep dish, mixed with butter, pepper, and salt.

~ Eliza Leslie, <u>Directions for Cookery, in its Various Branches</u>, 1848

Corn Fritters

1 cup flour
1/2 teaspoon cream
   of tartar
1/4 teaspoon baking soda
2 eggs
1/2 cup milk
2 cups corn, cut and
   scraped from the cob
Salt and pepper to taste
Lard for frying

Mix all ingredients together in a bowl, except for lard. In a skillet, melt the lard enough to cover the bottom of the skillet. Pour batter in skillet, a spoonful for each fritter. Fry until golden brown. Drain well. Serve immediately, with honey or molasses.

~ The Homeplace Recipe ~

Tennessee Fried Corn

fresh corn (6 ears will serve 6 people)
salt
3 tablespoons bacon drippings
butter
1/4 cup rich cream or milk

Select tender ears of corn. Cut kernels, not too close to the cob, then scrape the milky part off the cob. Add a little salt with one/half cup hot water.  Place corn in hot skillet with three tablespoons bacon drippings. Cook seven minutes. Add a lump of butter the size of a good egg and one-fourth cup cream or milk. Set to low heat to form a crust.

~ The Homeplace Recipe ~

In 1850, "molasses" meant "syrup." Homemade molasses was produced on the farm from apples and pumpkins, as well as corncobs.

❖ *We are trying to make some Molasses to day but it is a good deal of trouble, but I think if we were fixed for it, that it could be done easily.*

~ August 19, 1857, Diary of Jane M. Jones

Corncob Molasses

Makes about one pint

8 corncobs
4 cups water
1 pound brown sugar
   (3 cups)

In a kettle, cover the corncobs with water, and bring the water to a boil over moderate heat. Simmer for about forty-five minutes. Remove the corncobs and strain the liquid into a two and one/half to three quart saucepan. Add the sugar, and bring the liquid to a boil over moderate heat, and simmer, stirring and washing down the sugar crystals that cling to the side of the pan with a brush dipped in cold water until the sugar is dissolved. Cook the syrup over moderately high heat for ten to fifteen minutes until a candy thermometer registers 220°. Pour the molasses into a sterilized one-pint Mason-type canning jar and seal the jar with the lid. The corncob molasses will keep indefinitely in a cool, dry, dark place.

~ The Homeplace Recipe ~

The Institution of Pie

The pie is an English institution which, planted on American soil, forth-with ran rampant and burst forth into an untold variety of genera and species.

~ Harriet Beecher Stowe

Chess Pie

1 1/2 cup sugar
1/2 cup butter
1/4 cup milk
1 teaspoon cider vinegar

1 tablespoon cornmeal
3 eggs
1 teaspoon vanilla

Mix sugar and cornmeal. Melt butter and mix well with sugar. Add eggs one at a time and mix well after each; this is very important. Add milk, vanilla, and vinegar, beat well and pour in unbaked pie crust. Bake in quick oven, 400 degrees for ten minutes, then bake thirty minutes in moderate oven 325 degrees.

~ The Homeplace Recipe ~

When available, most sweet desserts at The Homeplace were made with dark, thick molasses, a syrup by-product of the sugar refining industry which families between the rivers in 1850 generally bought in barrels at the general store. The sorghum molasses produced in quantity in The Homeplace region at the turn of the century was almost unknown before the Civil War.

Molasses Custard Pie

Makes one 9-inch pie (6-8 servings)

1 recipe pie paste for a single crust pie (see next recipe)
1 1/2 cups unsulphured molasses
3/4 cups butter
1/2 cup heavy cream
3 eggs
Lard, butter, or bacon drippings

Make the pastry, press it into a lightly buttered nine-inch pie plate, and put it in the refrigerator to chill while you make the filling.

Preheat the oven to 400°.

Pour the molasses into a two quart saucepan and bring it to a boil over moderate heat. When it boils, remove molasses from heat and add butter. Stir until the butter has melted.

Add the cream to the molasses mixture and whip with a fork or a wire whisk for five minutes (or two minutes with an electric mixer). Add the eggs, one at a time, beating well after each addition.

Pour the filling into the prepared pastry shell and bake the pie in the center of the oven for ten minutes. Lower the oven temperature to 325° and continue baking for thirty-five to forty minutes, or until a knife blade inserted in the center of the pie comes out clean. Serve warm or at room temperature.

~ The Homeplace Recipe ~

In the 1850s, pie crust was called paste. The cookbooks of the 1800s suggested that a mixture of butter and lard rubbed into flour produced the flakiest crust. The flour was not modern all-purpose white flour or whole-wheat flour. The flour was soft wheat flour, finely sifted to remove most of the dark bran and germ, which contributed to quick spoilage. Today, all-purpose flour may be substituted.

Pie Paste 2

For a one-crust pie:

1 1/2 cups all-purpose flour
1/4 cup butter
1/4 cup lard
3-4 tablespoons cold water

For a two-crust pie:

2 cups all-purpose flour
1/3 cup butter
1/3 cup lard
4-6 tablespoons cold water

Combine the flour, butter and lard into a large mixing bowl. With the tips of your fingers, rub the flour and fat together until they resemble flakes of coarse meal. Add the cold water all at once, toss the mixture together with your fingers, and form into a ball. If it crumbles, add a little more water. Lightly butter a nine-inch pie plate. On a lightly floured surface, roll the dough (or slightly more than half of the dough if you are making a two-crust pie) into a circle about twelve inches in diameter.

Lift the circle of dough onto the rolling pin and unroll it carefully in the pie plate. Press it gently in place. For a one-crust pie, trim the overhanging edge about one half inch from the rim of the plate and tuck this overhang under to make it even with the rim of the plate. Finish the edge decoratively by scalloping it or crimping it with your fingers. For a two-crust pie, trim the overhanging edge even with the rim of the plate.

For the top crust, roll the reserved dough into a circle the same size and thickness as the bottom crust. Lift it onto the rolling pin and drape it gently over the filling. Trim the overhanging edge of the dough about one-half inch from the edge of the pie plate. Tuck this overhang under the edge of the bottom crust. Finish the edge decoratively by scalloping it or crimping with your fingers. Prick holes in the top crust with a fork to vent the steam. Bake according to the directions for individual pies.

~ The Homeplace Recipe ~

> ...of all fruits, no other can pretend to vie with the apple as the fruit of the common people.
>
> ~ Henry Ward Beecher

Apple Pie

Makes one 9-inch pie (6-8 servings)

1 recipe pie paste for a double pie
6 cups (about 2 1/2 pounds) tart, tender apples
1 tablespoon all-purpose flour
1 cup brown sugar
1/2 teaspoon ground cinnamon
1/4 teaspoon ground cloves
1 tablespoon butter, broken in small bits
Heavy cream

Make the pie paste, and line a lightly buttered 9-inch pie plate with one half of it. Put the other half in a covered bowl, and put both bowl and pie plate in the refrigerator to chill while you make the filling.

Preheat the oven to 350°.

Peel the apples, then quarter them, cut out the cores, and slice them one-fourth-inch thick.

Line the bottom pie crust with a layer of apples. Strew the layer with one third of the brown sugar and one third of the flour. Repeat twice. Sprinkle the spices over the top and dot with butter. Adjust the top crust, and bake the pie in the center of the oven for about forty minutes until the crust is golden brown. Serve warm in bowls with heavy cream.

~ The Homeplace Recipe ~

Mulberries are dark purple and look like elongated blackberries. They ripen in mid-June, and if you can beat the birds to the trees, you can make mulberry pies. Mulberries were not made into jams and jellies because they lack enough natural pectin.

Mulberry Pie

Makes one nine-inch pie (6-8 servings)

1 recipe pie paste for a double crust pie
4 cups mulberries
1 cup brown sugar
1/2 cup all-purpose flour
2 tablespoon butter, cut in small pieces,
and 1 tablespoon butter, melted

Preheat the oven to 400°.

Make the pastry, and line a buttered pie plate with one-half of it. Set aside the remaining half. For the filling, combine the mulberries, the sugar, and the flour in a large bowl, and mix them together gently but thoroughly. Scrape the contents of the bowl into the pie shell, mounding it higher in the center than at the sides. Dot the top of the filling with the two tablespoons of butter. Arrange the top crust, brush it evenly with the melted butter, and cut two vent holes for steam to escape with the tines of a fork. Bake the pie in the center of the oven for about 40 minutes until the crust is golden brown. Serve warm or at room temperature with heavy cream.

~ The Homeplace
Recipe ~

Summer Fruit Cobblers

Fruit Cobbler 1

Serves 6 to 8 people

1/2 cup butter
1 cup self-rising flour
  (or all-purpose flour and 1 1/2 teaspoon baking powder)
1 cup sugar
1/2 cup milk
1 large can fruit or pie filling and use only 1/2 cup sugar

Melt butter in pan. Mix flour and sugar together, add milk. Pour into pan of melted butter. Spoon fruit on top. Do NOT mix. Bake at 350 degrees for 25 to 30 minutes. Great recipe to use in a Dutch oven.

~ The Homeplace Recipe ~

Fruit Cobbler 2

Pie crust for 2 pies
4 to 5 cups fresh fruit pealed, seeded, sliced
1/2 cup to 1 cup of brown or white sugar, depending on
    sweetness of the fruit
2 to 4 tablespoon butter
1 teaspoon vanilla or other spices to taste

Mix fruit, sugar, butter and, spices together. Roll out pie dough. Line the bottom of a baking dish with a layer of pie dough (does not have to be neat). Put one/half of the fruit mixture over the pie dough. Then put another layer of pie dough, again does not have to be neat, can be pieces of dough laid side by side. Pour the remaining fruit mixture over the second layer of pie dough. Put a third layer of pie dough on the top; if this is one piece, cut in slits or strips of dough arranged decoratively. Bake at 350 degrees for twenty-five to thirty minutes until dough is brown and fruit is bubbly.

~ The Homeplace Recipe ~

Preservation Recipes

Vegetables and fruits preservation began in the early summer for winter use by either drying, pickling, sugaring or salting. Vegetable and crop varieties were open pollinated, so the seeds could be saved from one year to the next, thus having a local variety that adapted to the local environment. Along with salt, sugar, and vinegar, herb and spices such as sage, thyme, cinnamon, allspice, ginger, and nutmeg all have properties that discourage growth of bacteria in food.

The goal of preservation then as now is to limit the growth of bacteria and other micro-organisms that will spoil preserved food. Herbs and spices used in preservation not only add flavor but have antibacterial and microbial properties that aid in preventing spoiling of precious winter food stores.

~ <u>American Household Botany</u>

Beets Preserved in Brine

Pull small young beets and cook in hot water until skins pull off. Cool. Meanwhile, dissolve one cup salt, one-half cup vinegar and one-fourth cup sugar in two quarts boiling water. Pour over beets and let cool, then cover and place in cold room.

~ The Homeplace Recipe ~

Salted Green Beans

Take young beans gathered on a dry day, have a large stone jar ready, lay a layer of salt at the bottom, and a layer of beans, then salt, and then beans, and so on till the jar is full; cover them with salt and tie a coarse cloth over them and a board on that, and then a weight to keep it close from all air; set them in a dry cellar and when you use them, take some out and cover them close again; wash those you took out very clean, and let them lie in salt water twenty-four hours, shifting the water often; when you boil them do not put any salt in the water.

~ The Homeplace Recipe ~

Pickled Green Beans

Take young green beans, string them, but do not cut them in pieces. Put them in salt and water for 2 days, stirring them frequently. Then put them in a kettle with grapevine or cabbage leaves under, over, and all round them (adding a little piece of alum). Cover them closely to keep in the steam and cook them over slow heat till they are a fine green.

Having drained them in a sieve, make for them a pickle of cider vinegar, and boil it for 5 minutes; some mace, whole pepper, and sliced ginger tied up in a thin muslin bag. Pour it hot upon the beans, put them in a stone jar, and tie them up.

~ The Homeplace Recipe ~

Squash Pickles

6 to 8 squash (cut into small
　　pieces)
1 green sweet pepper,
　　chopped
1 red sweet pepper, optional
1 medium onion, chopped
Soak in ice cold water
　　for 2 hours, drain

Heat the following:

3 cups vinegar
3 cups sugar
1 teaspoon mustard
1 teaspoon celery seed
1 teaspoon turmeric
1/2 teaspoon pepper

Boil the above liquid, add vegetables, boil 3 minutes. Pack in
jars or crocks.

~ The Homeplace Recipe ~

Okra Pickles

3 1/2 pounds small okra pods
1 pint cider vinegar or distilled vinegar
1 quart water
1/3 cup canning salt
2 teaspoon dill seeds
garlic
hot pepper to taste

Pack okra firmly in jars or crock, put small piece of garlic in each. Make a brine of the vinegar, water, salt and dill seed. Pour boiling brine over okra and seal in jar or crock.

~ The Homeplace Recipe ~

Watermelon Rind Pickles

7 pounds watermelon rind, peeled
2 1/2 quarts of water
1/3 cup salt
6 1/2 cups brown sugar
2 cups vinegar
1 cup water
1 tablespoon cloves, whole
2 sticks cinnamon
2 lemons

Pare off the outer green from watermelon rind and cut in 1 inch squares. Put in large bowl and pour over them the salt and water mixed. Let soak for 3 days. Drain and let stand in fresh water for one hour. Make a syrup of sugar, vinegar water and spices. Cut the lemon (rind and all) paper thin. Put melon and lemon into hot syrup and boil until watermelon is clear. Seal in jars.

~ South Union Shaker Receipt ~

Sauerkraut

"If you have a big crop of cabbage, it is economical to cure it in brine, to make sauerkraut. The fermented vegetable serves as a 'pickle' and brings variety to winter meals when fresh vegetables are not always abundant."

"Remove and discard outer leaves from firm, matured heads of cabbage. Wash, drain, cut in halves or quarters and remove and discard cores. Shred 5 pounds cabbage at a time with a shredder or sharp knife. It should be no thicker than a dime."

Stone-Jar Sauerkraut

Prepare 40 to 50 pounds cabbage... To each 5 pounds of shredded cabbage add 3 1/2 tablespoon canning salt. Mix thoroughly. Pack firmly and evenly with a potato masher into a stone jar (or crock) that has been washed in soapy water, rinsed and scaled.

Repeat shredding and salting cabbage until jar is filled to within 5" from top. Press firmly (do not pound) with masher to extract enough juice to cover cabbage by the time jar is filled. Keep cabbage covered with juice.

Cover with two or three layers of white, clean cloth, tucking edges down against inside of jar. On top, place a scaled, heavy plate that just fits inside the jar.... Weight it down with a jar filled with water (or with a stone - not limestone...) so the juice comes over the plate.

Fermentation will begin the day following the packing. It works

faster at high temperatures and the kraut is more likely to spoil at a high temperature. The best quality product is made at room temperature (70 degrees).

Give kraut daily care. Remove the film as it forms and wash and scald the cover cloth as often as necessary to remove mold and film. When bubbling stops (in 2 or 3 weeks - or 4 weeks in cold weather), tap jar or crock gently. If no bubbles rise, fermentation has ended. Cover. Keep kraut in stone jar in cold room through the winter.

~ Farm Journal's Country Cookbook

To Pickle Cucumbers

Select a sufficient quantity of the size you prefer, which probably can be done at one time. Put them in a stone pot and pour over them a strong brine; to this add a small bit of alum, to secure the colour. Let stand a week; then exchange the brine for clear water, in which they must remain two or three days. Boil the best northern cider vinegar and when nearly cool, pour over the cucumbers, having previously turned off the water. Prepared in this manner, with the addition of cloves, allspice, mustard, and cinnamon, boiled in the vinegar, pickles of every kind will keep for a year. In pickling cauliflower, tomatoes, and other vegetables which easily absorb the vinegar - the spiced vinegar should be added when cold.

~ Phineas Thornton, <u>The Southern Gardener and Receipt Book,</u> 1845

The modern world calls the 1850s peach pickles, pickled peaches. They are wonderful as both a dessert and a garnish for meats.

Peach Pickles

Makes two quarts

12 medium-sized ripe peaches (about 3 pounds)
24 whole cloves
3 cups light brown sugar
1 cup cider vinegar
2 2-inch pieces of cinnamon stick
2 cups water

Plunge the peaches into a kettle of boiling water for one minute, drain, and peel. Insert two whole cloves in each peach.

Put the vinegar, sugar, the two cups of water, and the cinnamon sticks in a four to six quart kettle and bring the liquid to a boil over moderate heat. Add the peaches and simmer for about five minutes until they are just tender. Transfer the peaches to hot, sterilized, wide-mouthed Mason-type canning jars, packing them tightly, and put one cinnamon stick in each jar. Pour the hot syrup over the peaches, and seal immediately, according to manufacturer's instructions. Set aside in a cool place for at least three days before serving.

~ The Homeplace Recipe ~

❖ *Busy all morning make sweet pickle (peaches).*
Mr. G busy at his tobacco.

~ September 6, 1858, Diary of Betty Gleaves

Fruit Paper or Leather

To preserve fresh fruit, like peaches, apples, and tomatoes. Peel, remove seeds. Cook, stirring constantly over a low heat. When it is very thick, spread very thin layer on plates to dry in the sun. It should dry in 2-3 days. When dry, cut into stripes, roll up and store in jars. To use in winter, put pieces of leather into clean water and slow boil until a sauce. It can be used to make fruit pies, preserves, or as a snack.

~ The Homeplace Recipe ~

❖ *Assist Mr. G fan out some wheat on his new fan he got-- then go blackberry hunting.*

~ July 5, 1859, Diary of Betty Gleaves

❖ *Prepare some fruit to preserve--go over to see Mr. Gleaves' tobacco barn*

~ September 3, 1858, Diary of Betty Gleaves

❖ *Make my preserves and some for Cindy.*

~ September 4, 1858, Diary of Betty Gleaves

While modern cooks have the advantage of adding packaged pectin to take the guesswork out of gelling, a woman in the 1850s would have known when jam was ready to gel by the way it feels against the spoon. This skill can be acquired through practice.

Blackberry Jam
(or any fresh fruit)

5 cups blackberries
5 cups granulated white sugar

Gather blackberries when they are dark purple and very ripe, but include a handful of under-ripe berries to help the jam gel.

Rinse the berries quickly under running water and put them into a 4-6 quart enameled kettle. Crush them well with a wooden beetle or a potato masher. Bring to a boil over low heat, stirring frequently. Add the sugar, stir, and bring to the boil again, stirring frequently. Simmer until thick, remembering the jam will also thicken when it cools. To test thickness, drop hot jam into cold water, if it forms a soft ball it is finished. The cooking time varies from fifteen to forty minutes, depending on the character of the fruit.

Pour in small crocks, cover preserves with layer of beeswax and close tightly with cloth cover. Today preserves can be packed in hot, sterilized Mason-type jars, following the manufacturer's instructions for processing.

~ The Homeplace Recipe ~

Fruit Preserves

Take an equal portion of fruit and sugar and mix well. Cook over a medium heat until mixture drops off a wooden spoon in two places, usually 30 to 45 minutes.

~ The Homeplace Recipe ~

For pickling, gather walnuts when they are nearly full-size but before the shells has begun to harden. Only if the nuts can be pierced through with a needle are the nuts young and tender enough to pickle.

Pickled Walnuts

Makes one quart

4 cups young white walnuts (butternuts)
3 walnut leaves
1/4 teaspoon nutmeg
1/4 teaspoon mace
1 teaspoon salt
2-3 cups apple cider vinegar
water

Place the nuts in a 4-quart kettle, cover with boiling water, let stand for about a minute, and then drain. Rub off the fuzz on the outside of each nut with your fingers.

Return the nuts to the kettle, cover with three quarts of water, and bring to a boil over high heat. Simmer until the water turns to dark brown, then drain, add fresh water, and boil again. Keep boiling and draining off the discolored water until the water remains clear.

Put the drained walnuts into a one-quart, hot, sterilized Mason-type canning jar and cover them with the walnut leaves. Bring the vinegar, the spices, and the salt to a boil, and pour it over the walnuts to fill the jar within one fourth inch. Seal at once, following the manufacturer's instructions for processing. Let the walnuts pickle at room temperature for at least one month before serving.

~ The Homeplace Recipe ~

Tomatoes are native fruits of South America. Colonial Americans were cautious about tomatoes as possibly poisonous, though Thomas Jefferson did grow tomatoes in his gardens. As the following quote shows, tomatoes were considered an acceptable food by the mid-1800s:

"It (the tomato) is cultivated the length and breadth of the country. As a culinary dish it is on every table from July to October. It is brought to the table in an infinite variety of forms, being stewed and seasoned, stuffed and fried, roasted and raw, and in nearly every form, palatable to all. It is also made into pickles, catsup, and salted in barrels for winter use, so that with a few years more experience, we may expect to see it as an every day dish from January to January."

~ Robert Buist, The Family Kitchen Gardener, New York, 1847

Ripe Tomato Ketchup

2-3 green peppers
1 peck tomatoes (2 gallons)
3 pods red hot peppers to taste
6 onions
1quart cider vinegar
3 pints sugar
1 teaspoon each or to taste, allspice, cloves, and cinnamon

Chop tomatoes, peppers, and onions. Mix with other ingredients. Cook over medium heat. Stir often as the ketchup thickens. Cook until desired thickness.

~ The Homeplace Recipe ~

Surviving the Dog Days
with Prayer and Watermelon

The hot days of July and August are called the dog days from an ancient belief by the Greeks and Romans that Sirius, the dog star, was the cause of the hot weather. In the nineteenth century, the dog days brought on fevers and other maladies. We know today that these illnesses were mostly caused by bad waste management.

❖ *Go up to Mrs. Andrews. My Bible lesson comes…Cindy Murray comes down. Have nice watermelon from Mr. Pucket's. Peter comes from Mother's--she not well.*

~ August 20, 1859, Diary of Betty Gleaves

A Kentucky and Tennessee Folk Riddle

Here sits a green house.

Inside the green house is a white house.

Inside the white house is a red house.

Inside the red house

is a whole play party of white and black children.

What is it?

Answer: a watermelon

Watermelon

Take a fine ripe watermelon,

Cut out the soft part of it,

Leaving all the white part of the meat that is firm;

Cut them into any fanciful figure you please;

Put them into strong salt and water,

And let them remain in it for ten days;

Then soak them in fresh water three days,

Changing the water once a day,

And put them into a jar of strong vinegar,

With a little pepper, mace, and cloves.

They may be colored green with vine leaves,

Or red with beet juice,

And either makes a pretty garnish for meats.

~ Lettice Bryan, The Kentucky Housewife, 1839

Farm women learned from their mothers what plants could be used to cure illnesses brought on by the dog days. Maladies such as fevers, sores, insect bites, sore throats, coughs all could be treated by local plants that were made into teas or cooling compresses. Dogwood bark, which contains quinine, could be used to treat malaria. Violets, yarrow, golden rod, and Joe-Pye weed were used to treat typhoid fever. Sore throats could be treated with teas made from sumac berries, purple cone flowers, and yarrow. For the many skin aliments, from insect bites to sores to muscle strains and sprains, cooling compress were made from violets, chickweed, yarrow, jewelweed, and passion flower.

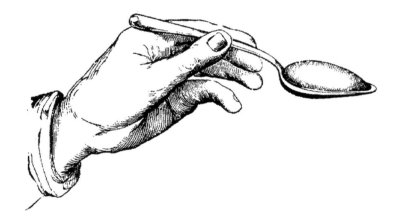

If the youngest child in a family sneezes at the dining table, there will be a death in the family.

~ Kentucky and Tennessee folklore

Notes for Your Homeplace

❖ *Well, I got up early and iced my cake. It looks very nice. All the young people came. I had a nice supper and then ice cream and fruit.*

~ August 11, 1856, Diary of Jane M. Jones

❖ *Nearly all the young people staid all night. I got up early. Had a nice breakfast. Never saw young people eat...like they did.*

~ August 12, 1856, Diary of Jane M. Jones

FALL

❖ *Indoors most all day - go out in evening & get some chestnuts.*

~ October 8, 1859, Diary of Betty Gleaves

❖ *It is quite cool cloudy and damp notwithstanding. We all fix up to go into the Fair. We spent a pleasant day. I got the premium on egg plants and grapes, Mr. Jones on his carriage horses.*

~ October 22, 1857, Diary of Jane M. Jones

❖ *Heard 2 or 3 steam boats passing the first this season.*

~ December 2, 1858, Diary of Samuel Stacker

With fall at The Homeplace came cooler weather and a busy time with the fall harvest. Fall garden vegetables were the same spring plants that liked cooler weather, but were different varieties. The fall varieties were larger in size than spring varieties, when these larger fall vegetables lost moisture in winter storage, then they would still be able to be used. Root crops would be stored in root cellars or buried in barrels or trenches in the garden. Some root crops were left in the garden and covered with straw to be dug later.

Work bees and frolics were held to help with the endless harvesting and preparing the food for storage. Corn-husking bees were fun for young people who were always hoping for a red cornhusk. Snap Apple (All Hallows Eve) was a time for games and spooky stories. In this section, you can join in and hear an old grandmother tell the story of "The Time Jack Tricked Old Scratch."

You can also join in with the preparation and celebration of a Homeplace wedding, even making a Bride's Cake. Weddings were held any time of the year, often when the circuit-riding preacher visited the community.

Hog killing was generally done between harvest and Christmas, which would give the family plenty of pork for the Christmas celebrations to come. The bounty of the harvest was celebrated with a traditional harvest feast for family and friends that would later become our national Thanksgiving holiday.

Join us now at The Homeplace for work, celebrations, and lots of frolics and foods.

Some Fall Dinners

The first time you hear a katydid, count six weeks ahead to know when it will first frost.

~ Farm folklore

Rabbit was always welcome addition to the table as a fresh meat and because it meant one less rabbit eating the vegetables in the garden.

Rabbit with Cream Gravy

Makes four servings

1-1 1/2 pound fresh rabbit, cut into serving pieces,
   or commercial ready-to-eat rabbit
1/4 cup all-purpose flour
3/4 teaspoon salt
Freshly ground black pepper
2 tablespoon lard or bacon drippings
1/2 cup chopped onion
3/4 cup water
1 tablespoon vinegar
1/3 cup heavy cream

Mix the flour with the salt and a few grindings of pepper in a shallow dish. Wash the pieces of rabbit under running water and dry them thoroughly. Dip each piece of rabbit into the flour mixture, and shake off the excess flour.

Melt the lard over moderate heat in a skillet large enough to hold all the pieces of rabbit. When the lard is hot, but not smoking, add the rabbit pieces and brown them slowly over moderate heat, about six minutes on each side. Sprinkle them with the onion, and pour in the water and vinegar. Cover the skillet and lower the heat, and simmer gently for about fifty minutes until the rabbit is tender. Remove the rabbit to a heated serving dish. Add the cream to the liquid remaining in the skillet. Heat it slowly until it has warmed through, but do not let it boil or it will curdle. Pour the gravy over the rabbit on the dish and serve at once.

~ The Homeplace Recipe ~

Cindy's Homeplace Chicken Pie

Boil a whole chicken, put in kettle, cover with water, and add one teaspoon salt. When tender and meat is falling off the bone, take the chicken out of the kettle and put on a plate to cool. Add to the broth, cut up pieces of potatoes and carrots or any other vegetables you want and add pepper to taste. When vegetables are soft, but still a bit firm, thicken the broth by adding a tablespoon of flour to 1/4 cup of water, stir and add to broth, let boil until thickened. Let broth cool down a bit and add chopped up pieces of chicken. Carefully spoon the warm thickened broth, chicken and vegetables into a pie shell and cover with another piece of pie dough. Bake at 400 degrees for twenty-five to thirty minutes until top is golden brown.

~ The Homeplace Recipe ~

Pork Roast and Dressing

1 pork roast   3 cups cornbread, crumbled
3 eggs   1 tablespoon sage
1/2 cup chopped onion

Mix cornbread, eggs, sage, and onion to make dressing. Put roast in roasting pan, season with salt and pepper. Put dressing around the roast. Bake at 350 degrees until the dressing is done and roast is golden brown and tender. Bake an hour to an hour and a half, depending to the size of the roast.

~ The Homeplace Recipe ~

Fruits and Vegetables

❖ *Kraut made today and buried cabbage.*

~ November 28, Diary of Samuel Stacker

Preservation of Cabbage

After they have got their growth, and are gathered in the fall, cut off their loose leaves and stalks, that nothing remains but the sound part of the head; they may be headed up in a tight cask. By thus excluding them from the air they may be kept for a long time. Those intended for the longest keeping should be put into small casks, as they will soon spoil when exposed to air.

~ Phineas Thornton, <u>The Southern Gardener and Recipt Book</u>, 1845

Folk wisdom warns not to pick persimmons until after the first frost. Though persimmons can ripen before frost, these fruits do ripen much later in the year than other fruits. According to folklore, the persimmon seed will foretell the weather. Break it gently in half. If the white kernel is in the shape of a knife, it means winter's cold will be cutting, a spoon shape means there will be plenty of snow to shovel, and a fork shape means a mild winter.

Persimmon Pudding

Makes six servings

3 cups ripe persimmons
1 egg
1 cup brown sugar
1 cup all-purpose flour
1 teaspoon baking soda
1/2 teaspoon salt
1/4 teaspoon cinnamon
4 tablespoon butter

The persimmons:

Gather persimmons in fall when their skin is wrinkled and the fruit is very soft; the insides should be mushy. The best test for ripeness is the taste test.

Remove the seeds by putting the peeled persimmons through a food mill or squeezing them through your fingers. Three cups of ripe persimmons will make about one cup of persimmon pulp.

The pudding:

Preheat the oven to 325°.

With one tablespoon of the butter, grease the bottom and sides of a one-quart baking dish.

Stir together the flour, baking soda, salt, and cinnamon in a small bowl. Set aside.

In a deep mixing bowl, beat the egg with a fork or wire whisk until it is light and frothy. Add the sugar and the persimmon pulp and stir until all ingredients are well combined. Add one-third of the flour mixture with one/third of the buttermilk and stir well. Repeat twice more, alternating the flour and the liquid in similar amounts.

Melt the remaining three tablespoons of butter in small pan over moderate heat and stir it into the batter. Pour the batter into the prepared pan. Bake in the middle of the oven for forty to fifty minutes, or until a knife blade inserted in the center of the pudding comes out clean. Serve warm or cold, with a brown sugar sauce.

~ The Homeplace Recipe ~

The recipe for brown sugar (or caramel) sauce is found with the Basic Cake in the Winter section.

Apple cider boiled until it reduces to a thick syrup could have been used as a sweetener for cakes, pies, and other desserts at The Homeplace when the molasses barrel was empty.

Apple Molasses

Fill kettle with apple juice (cider), boil, skimming frequently, till it becomes the consistency of cane molasses. Use for sweetening pies, dressings or puddings, etc.

~ Phineas Thornton, <u>The Southern Gardener and Receipt Book,</u> 1845

Apple Bread Pudding

Pare, core and slice thin a dozen or more apples strewing among them some bits of lemon rind that has been pared thin, and squeeze the juice of the lemon over the apples. Cover the bottom of a deep dish with a thick layer of sliced apples. Strew it thickly with brown sugar. Scatter on very small bits of the best fresh butter, then strew on a thin layer of grated bread crumbs. Continue this until you get the dish full, finishing with a thin layer of crumbs. Put into a moderate oven, bake pudding well, until the apples are done and soft as marmalade. Eat hot or cold, with cream sauce, or with butter, sugar, and nutmeg stirred to a cream. It will require for less baking, if the apples are stewed previously until soft and then mixed with the sugar and lemon and prepared as above. Grated nutmeg mixed with the apples will much improve the flavor.

~ Nineteenth-century Recipe

Baked Apples

Makes six servings

1 quart sweet apple cider
5 tablespoon butter
6 large tart, tender apples
1/2 cup walnuts or hickory nuts
1/2 cup brown sugar

Preheat oven to 375°.

In a three and one-half to four quart saucepan, bring the cider to a boil over moderate heat and boil it until it has reduced to one cup. Boil for about ten minutes more. Watch carefully and stir occasionally so that is does not scorch. Set the cider aside to cool.

With one tablespoon of the butter, butter the bottom and sides of a two-quart shallow baking dish. Remove the peel from the bottom third of the apples, core them, and place them in the baking dish, topsides down. Combine the brown sugar and the walnuts and 1 tablespoon of the boiled cider. Stuff the apples with this mixture, and top each apple with two teaspoons of butter.

Pour the rest of the boiled cider over the apples and bake them in the center of the oven, basting them every ten minutes with the syrup that collects in the bottom of the dish, for one hour, or until they are tender but not falling apart.

Serve the apples at once, or refrigerate, and serve cold.

~ The Homeplace Recipe ~

There was no such thing as seedless grapes in the 1850s, so dried grapes or raisins had to be seeded by hand.

Hasty Pudding

Boil a quart of entire sweet milk,
and stir into it while boiling enough thin flour batter,
made of milk and flour,
to make the whole as thick as good pudding batter.
Add a little powdered cloves and cinnamon,
a large spoonful of butter
and two ounces of sugar.
A handful of seed raisins or cherries would improve it.
Stir it constantly till done,
then serve it up in a bowl of suitable size,
sprinkle a handful of brown sugar over the top,
grate on a little nutmeg,
and send it to table warm.

~ Lettice Bryan, The Kentucky Housewife, 1839

Carrot Pudding

Boil tender, six carrots of middling size, pound, sift, and mix them with a pint of cream, sugar, spice and orange to the taste; bake in a dish lined with a thin, rich paste from thirty to forty five minutes.

~ A.L. Webster,
The Improved Housewife, 1858

Mulled Cider

Boil a quart of cider, with enough
cinnamon and cloves to flavor it,
and strain it through a napkin into a pitcher.
In the meantime beat six eggs light, and put them in a bowl:
Pour the cider while boiling on the egg, stirring in gradually;
add enough sugar to make it sufficiently sweet,
and whirl round in it a bunch of wire
till you raise a froth on the top;
then serve it up immediately
in glasses while it is warm,
and grate nutmeg thickly over them.
Wine may be mulled in a similar manner.

~ Lettice Bryan, <u>The Kentucky Housewife</u>, 1839

The nineteenth-century heirloom varieties of apple raised today at The Homeplace include Limbertwing, Horse, and Ben Davis. They have been carefully chosen so that their growing seasons overlap, providing fresh apples from August through October.

Fried Apples and Onions

Makes six servings

2 medium-sized onions (about 1 pound)
5 medium sized cooking apples (about 1 1/2 pounds)
4 tablespoons butter or bacon drippings

Peel the onions, cut them into one-fourth-inch slices, and separate them into rings. Peel the apples, quarter them, remove the cores, and slice about one-fourth-inch thick.

In a heavy, ten-inch skillet, melt two tablespoons of butter over medium heat. Add the onion rings and cook for about ten minutes, stirring occasionally, until they are limp and transparent. Transfer the onions to a plate and set aside.

Add the remaining two tablespoons of butter to the skillet and melt it over a medium heat. Add the apple slices and cook for three to four minutes, or until they are golden brown. Return the onions to the skillet, stir, and heat through, about thirty seconds.

Pile the apples and onions on a heated platter and serve at once.

~ The Homeplace Recipe ~

Ruta Baga
(Russian or Swedish Turnips)

This turnip is very large and of a reddish yellow color; they are generally much liked. Take off a thick paring, cut the turnips into large pieces, or thick slices, and lay them awhile in cold water. Then boil them gently about two hours, or till they are quite soft. When done, drain, squeeze and mash them, and season with pepper and salt, and a very little butter. Take care not to set them in the sun, or it will spoil the taste. *Russian Turnips should always be mashed.

~ Eliza Leslie, <u>Directions for Cookery, in its Various Branches</u> 1848

Direction for Boiling Potatoes

Seldom do we see potatoes well cooked and still more seldom do we see them cooked without waste. Choose your potatoes of equal size, put them in a pot without a lid, with enough water to cover  them, more water would spoil them, as the potatoes, on being boiled, yield a considerable amount of water by being boiled in a vessel without a lid. They do not crack and all waste is prevented. After the water has nearly come to boiling, pour it off, and replace the hot by cold water, into which throw a good portion of salt. The cold water sends the heat from the surface to the heart of the potato and makes it mealy…The only proper test of being done is trying with a fork….They will often crack when they are quite raw at the heart. After straining off water, they should be allowed to stand ten or fifteen minutes on the fire to dry.

~ Phineas Thornton, <u>The Southern Gardener and Receipt Book,</u> 1845

Turnip Tops

Put them into cold water an hour before they are dressed, the more water they are boiled in, the better they will look. If boiled in a small quantity of water they will taste bitter. When the water boils, put in a small handful of salt, then your vegetables, if fresh and young, about 20 minutes boiling will cook them, drain them through a skimmer. They are perhaps better when boiled with bacon.

~ Tennessee Farmer
(nineteenth-century farming journal)

The Homeplace Wedding

Of all the social gatherings, the wedding party was the jolliest. Everyone for miles around, colored or white, slave or free, was invited; and only serious illness or disaster of earthquake dimensions could prevent people from attending. Why not? For a wedding party combined about all the good features of every form of merrymaking. It could at times be a hunting party for the older women; it was a courting marathon for the young men and young ladies; it was a yarn-swapping contest for the old men; it was a continuous feat of the choicest of food, cooked by women who knew the art of cooking; it was always a dancing party after the wedding; and it was many other things too numerous to catalogue, all of which were somewhat livened by the "flowing bowl," or more accurately, the gurgling jug.

~ Frank Lawrence Owsley, Plain Folk of the Old South

If you are lucky enough to be visiting The Homeplace on the right day, you can be part of a traditional wedding celebration of the 1850s and even partake of a small piece of cake. If not, here is the recipe!

Frankly extravagant, this rich Bride's Cake was a special dish for a family living between the rivers in 1850. It receives raves at the wedding reenactments performed by Homeplace staff and volunteers. The recipe is little changed from the original published in The Kentucky Housewife in 1839. Rosewater, a fragrant solution made by distilling fresh rose petals in water, is responsible for the old-fashioned flavor.

The Bride's Cake

2 cups plus 1 tablespoon butter
2 cups granulated white sugar
1/4 cup white wine
1/3 cup brandy
1 tablespoon rosewater *(available at Middle Eastern and
    specialty food stores; you can use vanilla if preferred)*
1 teaspoon cinnamon
1/2 teaspoon nutmeg
1 tablespoon lemon juice
1/2 tablespoon grated lemon rind
4 cups pastry (cake) flour
Egg whites from 15 eggs

Preheat the oven to 350°.

With one tablespoon butter, grease the bottom and sides of a 9 x 3 1/4 inch cake pan. Combine the flour, cinnamon, and nutmeg, and sift them together onto a plate. Set aside.

In a deep bowl, cream the sugar and butter until the mixture is light and fluffy. Add (a small amount at a time) the wine, the brandy, the rosewater, the lemon rind, the lemon juice, and continue to beat until the ingredients are thoroughly combined.

Beat the egg whites until they are stiff and dry. Stir about one/third cup of the egg into the sugar-butter mixture. Add the flour mixture, about one/half cup at a time, beating well after each addition. Scoop the remaining egg whites over the batter and fold them gently but thoroughly together until no trace of white shows.

Pour the batter into the prepared pan, smoothing the top with a spatula. Bake in the center of the oven for one and one-half hours, or until a toothpick or a cake tester inserted in the center of the cake comes out clean and dry. Let the cake cool in the pan for about ten minutes, then invert it onto a wire rack to cool at room temperature. Frost when thoroughly cool.

Frosting

4 egg whites
4 cups confectioner's sugar
1 tablespoon lemon juice
1/2 teaspoon rosewater

Beat the egg whites until they are stiff and dry. Add the sugar, one/half cup at a time, the lemon juice, and the rosewater, and continue to beat until the egg whites are stiff and glossy.

Spread the frosting evenly over the top and sides of the cake. Decorate to your taste with real or artificial flowers.

~ The Homeplace Recipe ~
based on Lettice Bryan's recipe in <u>The Kentucky Housewife</u>, 1839

...The bride's cake was left dead-white, but it always stood on something footed, and had a wreath of evergreen and paper flowers, laid upon a lace-cut paper about the foot.

Baking it was an art. So many things had to go in it - the darning needle, picayune, ring, and button....They mixed the batter a trifle stiff, washed and scoured everything, shut eyes, dropped them, and stirred them well about. Thus nobody had the least idea where they finally landed - so the cutting was bound to be strictly fair. It made much fun - the bride herself cut the first slice - hoping it might hold the picayune, and thus symbolize good fortune. The ring presaged the next bride or groom, the darning needle single blessedness to the end, the thimble, many to sew for, or feed, the button, fickleness or disappointment. After the bridal party had done cutting, other young folk tempted fate....fragments of it, duly wrapped and put under the pillow, were thought to make whatever the sleeper dreamed come true. Especially if the dream included a sweetheart, actual or potential....

~ Martha McCulloch Williams,
Dishes and Beverages of the Old South,
1913

A picayune is a coin of small value.

Smokey, The Homeplace cat, possibly a descendent of many family cats, would be a welcome wedding guest!

It is good luck to have the family cat at a wedding.

~ Kentucky folklore

A wedding game used to determine the next bride was to toss the family cat on a quilt held by unmarried women. The women would hold the edges of the quilt, a cat was placed in the middle, and the quilt was lightly tossed to encourage the cat to run off. The women next to the cat as it ran off the quilt would be the next ones to be married.

Harmony

Cut up a pound of fresh butter and divide it in four equal parts.
Sift two pounds of flour, rub one portion of the butter into it,
with four ounces of powdered sugar;
make it into a very stiff dough with cold water,
and roll it into a thin sheet. Break up another portion
of the butter, spread it evenly over the paste with a broad
bladed knife, and sprinkle on a little flour; fold it up into a ball,
and roll it out again,
put on the other portions of butter
in the same manner as before, rolling it out each time; lastly
roll it into a sheet, cut it in circular pieces sufficiently large
to cover a small patty-pan, trim the edges smoothly,
crimp them neatly,
and bake them in rather a brisk oven.

Beat eight eggs very light, stir them into a quart
of rich sweet milk and boil it
till it becomes a curd,
stirring it up occasionally from the sides
to prevent its burning, then pour it in a sieve
and drain the whey from it.
Put the curd in a mortar,
add two ounces of butter, four of sugar,
a powdered nutmeg, a glass of white wine, the juice of a lemon
        and a few spoonfuls of sweet cream:
pound it till immediately united and very smooth; then
put a thick layer of it on each shell of paste,
        and pile whipped cream on the top.

~ Lettice Bryan, The Kentucky Housewife, 1839

And After the Wedding

An old story, originally of colonial New England origin, became popular all over the United States. Sometimes, the honeymoon is just over! So, it is said that a fisherman or some say a farmer went out daily to work the waters or soil and each noon and night when he came home, weary, his wife Anna served him the same meal of corn meal mush sweetened with molasses. Though he grumbled and grumbled, Anna never changed. Finally, the man couldn't eat the same meal one more time. So he grabbed his bowl of corn meal mush and molasses, threw in some flour and other ingredients, and angrily scraped it into a pan and baked it in a hot oven. All the while, he was heard to mutter, "Anna, damn her." When the bread was baked, he was delighted with the results. Some say the husband and Anna kissed and made up and shared the new bread, and well, some just don't say.

Anadama Bread

1/2 cup yellow corn meal
2 cups boiling water
2 tablespoons butter
1/2 cup molasses
1 teaspoon salt
1 pkg. active dry yeast,
    dissolved in 1/2 cup warm water
5 cups flour

Stir corn meal slowly into boiling water. When mixed, add butter, molasses, and salt. Cool to lukewarm. Add dissolved yeast and flour. Dough will be stiff. Knead well and keep in warm place. Let rise to more than double in bulk. Shape into two loaves and place in greased loaf pans. Let rise until light. Bake in 350 degree (quick oven) for one hour.

~ The Homeplace Recipe ~

Molasses Sweet Bread

Mix well 2 cups flour, 1 teaspoon cream of tartar, 1/2 teaspoon salt, 3/4 teaspoon soda, 2 teaspoons ginger, and 1 teaspoon cinnamon. Add to dry ingredients 1/3 cup butter, (melted if possible), 1 cup molasses, 3/4 cup buttermilk, and a slightly beaten egg. Pour in prepared loaf pan. Bake in moderate oven (350 degree) for fifty minutes. Cool ten minutes and turn out onto a plate.

~ The Homeplace Recipe ~

Snap Apple

❖ *Party.*

~ October 22, 1850, Diary of Jane M. Jones

❖ *Mother and I go to church. Mr. Thompson gave us an excellent sermon, "The eyes of the Lord are in every place beholding the evil & Good."*

~ October 30, 1859, Diary of Jane M. Jones

Snap Apple Night, better known to the modern reader as Halloween evening, would have been a good reason for a play party at The Homeplace. The families who lived at The Homeplace were largely descended from Scottish and Irish stock. Many of our Snap Apple (Halloween) customs come from these Celtic countries. This evening creates one of the thin places in Celtic lore where those spirits in the afterlife and other supernatural creatures are believed to visit the living, making this the perfect time for games that tell the future and scary stories around a fire! The fire kept the ghosts, goblins, and witches away!

Games for Snap Apple Night

One game of Snap Apple was set up with an apple suspended on a long string. The players tried to bite an apple - no hands allowed. Another version of the game was to fix an apple on one side of a stick and a lighted candle on the opposite side. The stick was then horizontally suspended while swung around. The object was to grab the apple between your teeth - not the candle!

Bobbing for Apples

Fill a large tub with water. Add however many apples you wish. The apples will then bob up to the water's surface. The players can only use their teeth to catch an apple. The first one to actually catch an apple wins. In ancient Celtic times, the first person, not already married of course, to catch an apple would be the next to marry.

…often the table was gay with autumn leaves, the center piece a riot of small ragged red chrysanthemums, or raggeder pink or yellow ones, with candles glaring from gorgeous pumpkin jack-o'lanterns down the middle….Often the bowl-tops were ornamented with leaves cut deftly from the skin of deep red apples.

~ Martha McCulloch-Williams,
Dishes and Beverages of the Old South, 1913

Snapping Apples:
Divining the Initials of a Future Husband
and All About Life

Peel a whole apple in as long a peel as possible. When the peel breaks throw it over your left shoulder. Whatever initial it falls into is the first initial of the person that you will marry. When the initial has been established, the seeds will tell you more about your future mate.

Cut an apple in half, then in quarters. Remove the seeds. Count them out according to one of these rhymes. The first is mostly done by girls, who had a vested interest in marrying well. The second could be done by boys.

<table>
<tr><td>

First:

One I love

Two I love,

Three I love I say,

Four I love with all my heart,

Five I cast away,

Six he loves,

Seven she loves,

Eight they both love,

Nine he comes,

</td><td>

Second:

Two means marriage

Three means a legacy,

Four means great wealth,

Five means long journey,

Six means great Fame.

Ten he tarries,

Eleven he courts and

Twelve he marries.

</td></tr>
</table>

The Time Jack Tricked Old Scratch

A Tale for Snap Apple

"Gather round the fire," the old grandmother said. As she was the best storyteller all around, all of the children, mothers and fathers, aunts and uncles, and even grandmothers and grandfathers gathered.

"On Snap Apple Night," the old grandmother said, "it's fitting to tell the story of how the jack o'lantern came to be. As she said this, a candle in the pumpkin on the porch of the double-pen house flickered. "In our homelands of Ireland and Scotland," she began:

"There lived our old friend, Jack, or perhaps he was the grandfather of the Jack we usually tell about, but he was also called Jack. Now, this Jack loved to play tricks on folks and besides this he didn't take up with any of these temperance speakers. Why, he could drink a cherry bounce, or something stronger, faster than a pig can squeal. Now, one night, as it happens Snap Apple Night, also called All Hallows Eve, when anybody with any sense knows that the wool between the worlds is thin, and spirits from the little people that cause little harm to Old Scratch, the Devil himself, roam the earth, Jack was out drinking at the local tavern.

And who should join Old Jack but Old Scratch, the Devil himself. "Time to join me, Jack," said Old Scratch.

"How about another cherry bounce before we go?" Jack asked, knowing that the Devil was always thirsty. The Devil agreed, but when it came time to pay, neither Jack nor the Devil had any money. "Hey," said Jack, "you can change yourself into a coin and show up in my pocket, and I can use you to pay for the drink, then you can shift back into your old handsome self."

Quick as a flash, Jack felt a coin in his pocket, but what the Devil didn't know was that Jack also carried a silver cross in that pocket. Now, the Devil was trapped. Jack said, "Okay, Old Scratch, if you promise to let me stay on earth another year, I'll let you out."

After the Devil had slunk off into the night, Jack made a prayer promising he'd quit drinkin' and fiddlin' and playing tricks on folks. But a year is a long time, and pretty soon, Jack was back to his old ways.

A year later, on the next Snap Apple Night, Jack was leaving that tavern, again full of cherry bounce, when suddenly right next to him Old Scratch was walking too. "Time to go, Jack," Old Scratch said, "and I am not turning into any coin or getting in any pocket."

"Fair enough," said Jack, but he noticed they had walked under a big apple tree. "But surely," said Jack, knowing that the Devil was always hungry, "we could each have a juicy apple before we go. You stand on my shoulders and pick us each an apple."

So, Old Scratch stood on Jack's shoulders to pick the apples, but before he could pick even one apple, Jack pulled his knife out of his pocket and cut crosses on the tree trunk. Now, that trapped the Devil and only the man who carved the crosses could release him. Old Scratch pleaded and begged to get down from the tree. Finally, Jack said, "If you don't take me for another ten years, I'll let you down."

As Old Scratch slunk off into the night mumbling that Jack was just as mean as a rattlesnake and he didn't want that soul in his place, Jack again promised in a prayer to live right. But ten years is a long time, and pretty soon, Jack was up to his old ways again.

But all that drinkin' and fiddlin' and tricking folks finally wore down Old Jack's body and before that ten years was even up, the cedar tree Jack had planted in his yard grew big enough to shadow a grave and Old Jack died. Jack just had time to grab one of the big turnips he had stored for winter when he was whisked up to the gates of Heaven. Saint Peter met Jack at the gates and said, "Sorry, Jack, but all your promises was as crooked as a dog's hind leg and all your doings was twice as dirty. I can't let you into Heaven."

Well, Jack thought, I guess I'll have to go lie with Old Scratch down below. Still toting his turnip, Jack soon arrived at the gates of Hell. The Devil himself met Jack at the gates and said, "Go away, Jack. I've had enough of your tricks and I don't want your soul."

Now, Jack was in a fix. He had nowhere to go but back to earth but he could no longer live there as a man. He could only wander the dark nights, perhaps seen on nights such as Snap Apple with only his turnip for company. He had even begun to carve a face on the turnip so he could talk to it. "For old time's sake," Jack begged the Devil, "give me a chunk of coal from your fiery furnace to help me light my way." To get Jack away from his gate, Old Scratch threw him a coal and it landed right in that turnip. Now, to this day, in that old country, folks put a light in a turnip on All Hallows Eve to signal to Old Jack to stay away from their houses.

But somehow, Jack followed some of us folks all the way to Kentucky and Tennessee and he was able to change that old turnip for a big pumpkin just ripe on the vine. He carved another face and to this day, on certain nights you can see those strange lights dancing near the waters and fields. Some folks call them will o'wisps, but now you all know that is Jack dancing with his pumpkin lantern. And to this day on Snap Apple Night, we all carve our own jack o'lanterns to keep Jack away from our houses, and to remember the story."

The candle in the jack o' lantern on the porch of double-pen house flickered again, and then everyone hurried inside to bob for apples and eat apple pie.

Jack liked his cherry bounce, as did George Washington!

Cherry Bounce

Mix together equal proportions of black hearts

and morella cherries, which must be very ripe,

and full of juice. Extract one half of the stones,

and break up the other half with the cherries.

Weigh the whole,

and to each six pounds add one gallon of rectified whiskey.

Put it in a cask, stop it closely,

and let it set in a cool place for two months,

shaking it up frequently for the first month.

Then draw off the liquor, strain it,

dissolve in it one pound of loaf sugar,

or of sugar candy,

to each gallon, and bottle it for use.

~ Lettice Bryan, The Kentucky Housewife, 1839

With apples sun-dried in the fall, families at The Homeplace had apple desserts all through the year.

Dried Apple Pie

Place four cups of dried apples and a few cranberries if desired in a large baking dish, cover with water and put in a 350 degree oven for an hour, add more water as needed, or slowly simmer on the stove top in a sauce pan. Pour off the liquid. Add to the apples and cranberries, sugar and cinnamon to taste. One tablespoon of lime juice, orange peel, or raisins can be added. Add mixture to a pie paste and bake in a moderate oven until dough is browned.

Other dried fruits can be substituted for apples.

~ The Homeplace Recipe ~

Today, we connect pumpkins with Halloween, and we rarely eat them except in pies. In 1850, pumpkins were prized for their keeping qualities and grown in quantity. Families between the rivers boiled them, baked them, fried them, dried them, and made pumpkin butter out of them.

Whole Baked Pumpkin

Makes about six servings

1 small pumpkin
  (2-3 pounds)
1 tablespoon plus 1
teaspoon butter
1/3 cup heavy cream
2 tablespoon brown sugar
1/2 teaspoon salt
1/8 teaspoon nutmeg

Preheat the oven to 350°.

With a small, sharp knife cut a circular opening in the top of the pumpkin about two inches in diameter keeping the stalk in the center. Pull this top section off the pumpkin and set aside. With the edge of a large, metal spoon, scrape the seeds and the stringy membrane from the inside of the pumpkin and discard them. Wash the pumpkin inside and out with cold, running water, and pat it dry with paper towels.

With 1 tsp. of butter, grease the bottom of a shallow baking pan slightly larger than the diameter of the pumpkin. Place the pumpkin in the pan. Pour the cream into the cavity of the pumpkin; add the butter, the brown sugar, and the salt, stir, and sprinkle with the nutmeg. Place the pumpkin top alongside the pumpkin (not on top of it) on the same pan.

Bake the pumpkin in the center of the oven for one hour and forty-five minutes, or until the insides are soft.

Remove from the oven and cool for five minutes. Transfer the pumpkin to a serving platter with a wide spatula. Replace the top positioning it so that it does not slip down inside the cavity.

To serve, spoon portions of the pumpkin flesh and the cream filling from the inside of the pumpkin. Be careful not pierce the outer skin of the pumpkin because the filling will leak out.

~ The Homeplace Recipe ~

Corn Shucking

Corn-husking bees were one of the many community bees that helped get work done at The Homeplace. Often, rival teams would compete to see who could finish first husking the corn from two even piles of ears of corn. A bonus for those of courting age was that if a young man husked a red ear of corn, he had the privilege of kissing the girl nearest him.

❖ *Have corn shucking. Good many to help.*

~ November 8, 1858, Diary of Betty Gleaves

If you love fun and frolic, and waste and slovenliness more than economy and profit, then give a husking. Sing dirty songs for the entertainment of the boys, and expect your corn to be mixed, crumbled, and dirty; some husked, some half husked, and some not at all.

~ Farmer's quote in <u>Shucks, Shocks, and Hominy Blocks:</u>
<u>Corn as a Way of Life in Pioneer America</u>
by Nicholas Hardeman

For large gatherings such as corn shucking bees, the guests would bring their own plates, silverware, and cups as the host family would not have owned enough of their own to serve everyone.

Shortbread

1 cup flour
3 tablespoons powdered sugar
1/2 cup butter

Combine, roll out or press with hand one/half inch thick, cut with biscuit cutter, or into squares with a knife. Bake at 350 degrees until lightly browned, about eight to ten minutes. These are like sweetened pie dough and best eaten with fresh strawberries or other fruit on top. Top everything with a big spoonful of whipped cream.

~ The Homeplace Recipe ~

Pleasing Sweet Potato Pie

1 1/4 cup strained mashed
   cooked sweet potatoes
3/4 teaspoon salt
1 cup, plus 1 tablespoon milk
2 eggs
3/4 cup sugar
3/4 teaspoon cinnamon
1/4 teaspoon nutmeg and ginger
2 tablespoons butter, melted

Bake in hot oven, 450 degrees. Beat all ingredients together. Pour into pie crust. Bake 45 to 55 minutes. Insert knife one inch from the side, if done the knife will come out clean. Center may look soft, but will set later.

~ The Homeplace Recipe ~

The following recipe is large and will make several cakes, nice unique flavor; a combination of a pound cake and yeast bread:

A Good Family Cake

2 pounds flour (8 cups)
1/2 pound butter (1 cup)
1/2 cup white sugar (2 cups)
1 pint of milk (2 cups)
3 eggs
1 gill of yeast
    (1 gill =1/2 cup, but modern equivalent is 4 teaspoons,
    or 2 packets of modern active dry yeast)
1/2 teaspoonful of mace
Spice to taste (vanilla, cinnamon, ginger, allspice, etc.)

Mix well 1/2 flour with yeast and warm milk and let stand until perfectly light. Add eggs, butter, sugar, and spice together, and stir in remainder of flour; then gently pour this into the first mixture. Let all stand till perfectly light, then put into your pans and bake.

~ The Homeplace Recipe ~

Pork: the Staff of Life

> Games's good as any relish and so's bread; but pork is the staff of life.
>
> ~ James Fenimore Cooper, <u>The Chainbearer</u>

❖ *Kill hogs today - 26...*

     ~ November 16, 1858, Diary of Betty Gleaves

❖ *Killed twenty hogs this morning. I expect to feast on fresh meat....*

     ~ December 6, 1850, Diary of Jane M. Jones

Hogs were one of the most important animals on a family farm in the mid-nineteenth century at The Homeplace. Despite the seemingly indifferent care, hogs were second only to tobacco as a source of income on farms in this area. Not only were they a source of cash, but they also furnished the farm with one of the staples of the southern diet: salt-cured pork. There was a strong movement to improve the breed of hogs raised in the south. Swine breeders took pride in their stock, importing lines from Europe and elsewhere. The Berkshire breed drew the most advocates. Other popular breeds included Essex, Poland China, Neapolitan, and Sussex swine. But it is doubtful that these imported breeds had much affect on hogs in farms such as The Homeplace in the Land Between The Rivers.

The practice of allowing hogs to forage in the wild for food placed a premium on swift, wary, long-nosed hogs. Hogs thrived in the state's mild climate, which supported rich, mast producing forests of chestnut, oak, and hickory, in addition to corn production. When improved breeds were introduced, they often became so intermixed with feral populations that the improved bloodline was diluted beyond recognition. Free-roaming pigs sometimes became feral and entered folklore as the wild razorbacks of the south.

The southern hogs are a queer breed… with their sharp, thin backs, long heads, and tall legs, looking so little like hogs…very wild…perfectly ownerless, swift of foot, and strong withal.

~ P.H. Gosse, Letters From Alabama (1859)

Tennessee and Kentucky were the most outstanding producers among the Southern states, but North Carolina, Georgia, Alabama, and Mississippi all ranked quite high. By the 1850s, Tennessee became the leading state in the nation for swine production. On the eve of the Civil War, Tennessee's hog population numbered about 1.5 million.

Number of swine by states and year

	1840	1850
Tennessee	2,927	3,105
Kentucky	2,311	2,891
Virginia	1,992	1,830
N. Carolina	1,650	1,813
Georgia	1,458	2,169
Alabama	1,424	1,905
Mississippi	1,001	1,583

Rendering Lard

Good homemade lard, the rendered fat from the hog, is one of the choicest fats the housewife can use. The leaf fat, back fat, and the fat trimmings are usually rendered together. The caul and ruffle fats from the offal yield a darker product and should be rendered separately. This fat which is obtained from the internal organs (killing fat) promptly chilled makes fair lard, but many prefer to use it as soap stock. All the lean meat should be trimmed out of the fat before it is rendered. If lean meat remains it drops to the bottom of the kettle and is likely to scorch and discolor the lard. Fat will render more rapidly and yield a higher percentage of lard if it is cut into small pieces of uniform size. It is not necessary to remove the skin, but many persons prefer to remove it and they run the pieces of fat through the coarse plate of the sausage grinder.

~ The Homeplace Recipe ~

Souse

The feet and ears of the hog are best for this, though the upper part of the head is often used, removing the fat where there is too much. To prepare the feet, scald them well: scrape off the hair. Some persons roll them in hot ashes: I prefer the boiling water, as the other plan frequently scorches the skin, and souse should be very white.

Scrape them, removing the horny part: when all are well cleaned, lay them to soak a day and night. Put them to boil in plenty of cold water: skim the pot well: simmer them gently. When the bones can be removed easily, take them up, and as soon as they can be handled, pick the meat from the bones; season the mass highly with salt, black pepper, red pepper, and sage; pack it in molds, and lay over each a clean cloth dipped in vinegar; dip the cloth in vinegar every day, and it may be kept for some time in that way, or it may be packed in jars and covered with half vinegar and water.

~ The Homeplace Recipe ~

Pork Souse Meat (Headcheese*)*

Feet can be used. Boil pig's feet separately from head, because it takes a different amount of time for feet and head to become tender. Remove the eyes and clean head real well. Remove all hair by scraping. Put in slight salt water and let stand overnight. Some receipts call to stand head in salt water for three days.

Cook head until good and tender, two hours or so. Let the head cool, then remove meat and gelatin from the head and feet. Send meat though sausage grinder. Add sage, black pepper, and red pepper, stir well. Put into mold or seal in crock jars. Slice and serve hot or cold.

~ The Homeplace Recipe ~

The "hog-killing" as an event was often a social occasion, with much hard work followed by a "feast" of fresh pork. When as many as 10-15 hogs were to be killed at one time, the cooperation of friends and neighbors for miles around was usually needed. Hog-killings were like other social events that centered around a communal chore.

❖ *Kill hogs today--26. Have severe toothache all day.*

~ November 16, 1858, Diary of Betty Gleaves

Slaughter hogs when the moon is waxing or the meat will shrink in the pot.

~ Farm folklore

Scrapple

Boil a fresh-killed hog's head tender. This is made in the winter during what we in the South call "hog-killing." Take it up and remove all bones: chop the meat very fine and season it with salt pepper, and sage, as sausage meat; strain the liquor; wipe the pot nicely; return the broth to the pot; there would be about a quart of this. Put the meat back and stir into the broth fine corn meal until the mass is the consistence of soft mush; let this simmer half an hour, stirring frequently; pour the mixture into pans three or four inches deep. When cold slice in thin slices, roll in corn meal or flour, and fry in boiling lard, a light brown. This keeps as well as souse; it should be well protected from dust and air.

~ Mrs. Hill's New Cook Book, 1867

Fresh Pork Sausage

4 pounds pork (1 part fat to 2 parts lean; grind meat fine)
4 level teaspoons ground sage
1/2 level teaspoon ground cloves
   or 1 level teaspoon ground nutmeg
5 level teaspoons salt
2 level teaspoons black pepper
1 level teaspoon sugar

Mix above ingredients; add to meat and stuff into bags (before stuffing bag soak bags in water). Hang in smokehouse and smoke with rest of meat.

~ The Homeplace Recipe ~

❖ *Get my lard all dried. My feet cleaned – sausage meat.*

~ November 16, 1858, Diary of Betty Gleaves

The feet referred to above are hogs' feet, also used in cooking! It would be hard to reproduce the curing process in a twenty-first century kitchen, but you can use the same ingredients, and the finished product is still far superior to most commercially sold sausage.

To Salt Meat

The recipe that we use to salt the pork hams, shoulders, and side meat (bacon) is:

Per 100 pounds of meat
8 pounds of pickling salt (non-iodized)
2 pounds of sugar
2 ounces of salt peter

Divide into three parts. Salt pork down well, making sure to rub salt into all of the curves of the meat, especially down into the joints of the hams, and shoulders. Set meat to drain. Three days later re-salt the meat and set it back to drain again. Three days later, salt again. After this salting, the meat should stop draining. Let sit for about six weeks.

~ The Homeplace Recipe ~

Very Fine Sausage

Having removed the skin, &c. from a nice, tender part of fresh pork, beat it exceedingly fine, with one-fourth its weight of the leaf fat.

Prepare some sage leaves, by drying and rubbing them though a sifter, season the meat highly with the sage, salt, cayenne, mace, powdered rosemary, grated nutmeg, and lemon. Work with your hand till it is very well incorporated, making it a little moist with water.

Stuff it into skins, which have been neatly prepared and soaked in vinegar and water for a few hours; or stuff into muslin sausage bags, hang them up, and smoke them and when you make use of them, cut them into links, and stew, fry or broil them.

Serve them up on small toast and pour a few spoonfuls of melted butter around them.

~ The Homeplace Recipe ~

Kraut and Backbone

Take backbone after hog killing, wash well. Place in a deep skillet and cover with kraut. Bake in moderate oven (350 degree) for about two hours.

Pork ribs can be cooked the same way as the backbone.

~ The Homeplace Recipe ~

On slaughtering day at The Homeplace, there was no time to fuss with fancy receipts. The spareribs the family had as a once-in-a-year treat were baked in the oven, basted with a simple vinegar-sugar sauce.

Baked Spareribs

Makes six servings

4 pounds pork spareribs
1/2 cup cider vinegar
1/4 cup brown sugar
2 teaspoons salt
Freshly ground black pepper

Preheat the oven to 350°.

Combine the brown sugar and vinegar in a small bowl. Cut the ribs into serving pieces and arrange them flesh side up on the rack of a roasting pan. Sprinkle them with the salt and a few grindings of pepper and brush them with the sauce. Bake in the center of the oven for one hour, basting two or three times with the remaining sauce, or until they are brown and crackling. Remove to a heated platter and serve at once.

~ The Homeplace Recipe ~

Homemade Sausage

Makes three pounds of sausage

2 pounds lean pork (shoulder or loin preferred)
1 tablespoon salt
1/4 teaspoon red pepper
1/2 teaspoon nutmeg
1 pound pork fat (backbone fat preferred)
1 1/2 teaspoons ground sage
1 teaspoon thyme
1 1/2 teaspoons freshly ground black pepper

Grind the pork lean and fat together in a food grinder, or have a butcher grind it for you. Put it into a large bowl, add the seasonings, and knead it with your fingers until all ingredients are thoroughly combined. Shape into three loaves of equal size, wrap each loaf in waxed paper, and refrigerate for several hours overnight. To cook the sausage, cut slices from the loaves about one/half inch thick. Brown in a skillet over moderate heat for four to six minutes; turn, and brown the other side. Cover the skillet, lower the heat, and cook for fifteen minutes more. Remove the sausage to a warm platter and serve immediately, with gravy if desired.

~ The Homeplace Recipe ~

Sausage Gravy

Drippings from frying sausage
1/2 teaspoon salt
Freshly ground black pepper

1 cup milk
1 tablespoon flour

Pour off all but a thin film of fat from the skillet. Stir in the flour and cook, stirring, for about one minute. Then pour in the milk in a slow stream, stirring constantly. Stir and cook over low heat until the gravy is thick and bubbly. Simmer for two to three minutes, then add the salt and a few grindings of pepper and pour over the hot sausage.

~ The Homeplace Recipe ~

Election Day

❖ *Today is the day for the presidential election, beautiful day.*

> ~ November 4, 1856, Diary of Jane M. Jones

❖ *This is the great Election day.*

> ~ November 6, 1860, Diary of Jane M. Jones

❖ *Mr. Jones goes to town, says Lincoln is elected President of these United State. I humbly pray it is all for the best.*

> ~ November 8, 1860, Diary of Jane M. Jones

In the original colonies, a New England custom was to celebrate Election Day. Especially in Connecticut, to sustain those waiting for the votes to be counted and out-of-town representatives, housewives made Election Cakes as early as 1771. By the nineteenth century, this tradition of baking Election Cakes had spread west and recipes are given in nineteenth-century cookbooks.

Election Cake

Take half a pint of lively yeast,

mix with it half a pint of sweet milk

and enough flour to make it a good batter;

cover it and set it by the fire to rise.

This is called setting a sponge.

Sift two pounds of flour into a bread pan,

Cut up in it a pound of fresh butter,

add a pound of powdered sugar,

two grated nutmegs

and six beaten eggs.

When the sponge is quite light, pour it on the flour &c.,

make the whole into a soft dough, knead it well,

and make it into small flattish loaves.

Sprinkle a shallow iron pan with flour,

lay the rolls in it close together,

put them at first in a very slow oven,

that will permit them to rise, and when risen,

bake them with moderate heat.

~ Lettice Bryan, <u>The Kentucky Housewife</u>, 1839

The Thanksgiving Debate

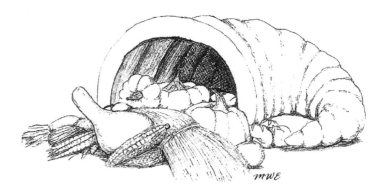

Thanksgiving through the first half of the nineteenth century was an uncertain celebration. Though George Washington proclaimed a national Thanksgiving Day in 1789, there was no regular national observance. Then, in 1827, Sarah Josepha Hale, the editor of the influential <u>Godey's Lady's Book</u> - this was the journal that told women how to do everything right - began an over-thirty-year campaign to have a permanent national holiday of Thanksgiving.

Women at The Homeplace who were able to read copies, perhaps borrowed or passed on, of <u>Godey's Lady's Book</u> would have been encouraged to prepare Thanksgiving dinners such as roast turkey with giblet gravy, creamed baby onions, and cranberry sauce the last Thursday in November as a day of patriotic thanksgiving. Hale regularly implored her readers in the 1850s to influence support for "this annual festival...the exponent of family happiness and household piety, which women should always seek to cultivate in their hearts and in their homes." It was not, though, until 1863 that President Abraham Lincoln proclaimed the last Thursday in November as a national holiday, Thanksgiving.

Thanksgiving

By Lillian

God of the rolling year's returning harvest,

A tribute to thy boundless love we bring,

Without whose gracious gifts the spirit starveth

And hope falls lifeless from its loftiest wing,

Thy rainbow-pledge, in living colors painted

On the cloud-shadowed arch of summer skies.

Though hast again redeemed; and ere, we fainted,

The year's life-boon was laid before our eyes.

With grateful hearts we praise thee for it Father;

Into thy presence with thanksgiving come;

And, as around thine alter we gather,

Smile on us from thine everlasting home!

We thank thee for the south wind's breath of gladness,

The genial sunshine of the spring's young hours,

That lifted winter's melancholy sadness

From off the ice-embosomed tomb of flowers.

~ <u>Godey's Lady's Book,</u>
October 1857

Notes for Your Homeplace

❖ *Put out sweet potatoes in the cellar.*

    ~ November 2, 1859, Diary of Betty Gleaves

❖ *Mr. Ford is filling the ice house.*

    ~ December 8, 1859, Diary of Jane M. Jones

❖ *Put potatoes in cellar and boiled greens.*

    ~ December 4, 1858, Diary of Samuel Stacker

CHRISTMAS

❖ *I staid the day with Cousin Mary to take care of her little boy. Cousin Robert and myself made some eggnog, which was very nice.*

~ December 25, 1850, Diary of Jane M. Jones

❖ *I am very busy fixing up little Christmas present for the children. The dear little ones are very much excited about it.*

~ December 24, 1856, Diary of Jane M. Jones

❖ *Well, a pleasant Christmas day.*

~ December 25, 1856, Diary of Jane M. Jones

The Christmas season was marked by firecrackers, general jollity, and above all feasting - turkeys dressed with oysters, baked hams, plum puddings with rich wine sauce and sillibub. Country people seldom had the last two or even oysters, but there were roasted geese and hams, plates of high stack-pies, with cakes of all description, and shotgun and anvil blasts added to the firecrackers.

~ Harriette Simpson Arnow in <u>Flowering on the Cumberland</u>

Southern backwoodsmen galloped home from their best girls' houses at Christmas firing pistols with wild abandon. So common was this practice in some southern communities that the erratic firing of a pistol by a single man was a sure sign of two things: he had either broken up with his girl, or he was going to get married right away.

~ Thomas D. Clark in <u>Pills, Petticoats, and Plows:</u>
<u>The Southern Country Store</u>

Egg Nog

Break six eggs, separating the whites from the yolks;

Beat the whites to a stiff froth,

put the yokes in a bowl and beat them light.

Stir into it slowly, that the spirits may cook the egg,

half a pint of rum, or three gills of common brandy;

add a quart of rich sweet milk

and half a pound of powdered sugar;

then sit in the egg froth, and finish

by grating nutmeg on the top.

~ Lettice Bryan, The Kentucky Housewife, 1839

If you had a fond and extravagant grandmother, you were almost sure to have also a clove apple. That is to say, a fine firm winter apple, stuck as full of cloves as it could hold, then allowed to dry very, very slowly, in air neither hot nor cold. The cloves banished decay - their fragrance joined the fruity scent of the apple, certainly set off things kept in the drawer with the apple. The applemakers justified their extravagance - by asserting a belief in clove apples as sovereign against mildew or moths…

~ Martha McCulloch-Williams, Dishes and Beverage of the Old South, 1913

Pink Syllabub

Stir gradually into a quart of rich sweet cream

a pint of white wine,

the juice of three lemons,

eight ounces of powdered loaf sugar,

a few spoonfuls of currant jelly,

and enough cochineal tincture or powder

to color it a fine pink.

Set it by for two or three hours,

then whip it to a froth,

and put it into glasses,

piling it high.

~ Lettice Bryan, The Kentucky Housewife, 1839

Cochineal is a food coloring made from crushed insects. According to Waverly Root in Food, Bernal Diaz, chronicler of Cortez's conquest of Mexico, first encountered cochineal in the Mexican markets. In the 1800s, it was a common food and dye coloring.

Hot Spiced Apple Cider

2 quarts apple cider
1/3 cup brown sugar
3 inches of a stick of cinnamon
1 teaspoon whole allspice
1 teaspoon whole cloves
1/4 teaspoon nutmeg

Pour cider into a three to four quart pan. Stir in the brown sugar and spices. Slowly bring the mixture to a boil. Cover and simmer two minutes. Remove the spices by straining the mixture. If you prefer, tie up the spices in cheesecloth, add the cheesecloth bag to the cider, and remove the bag before serving.

~ The Homeplace Recipe ~

Because fruit butters were made with no added sugar, they substituted for more expensive jams, jellies, and fruit preserves at The Homeplace. Pear butter is grainy and intensely sweet, fine for spooning on hot biscuits.

Pear Butter

Makes about 2 1/2 cups

6 ripe pears   3 cups sweet apple cider
1/8 teaspoon nutmeg   1/4 teaspoon ground cloves
1/8 teaspoon mace

Peel the pears, quarter them, remove the cores, and cut them in small pieces. Put them in a three quart saucepan, add the apple cider, and bring to a boil over high heat. Reduce the heat and simmer uncovered for about one hour, or until the pears are very soft. Mash the pears with a wooden "beetle" or a potato masher. Add the spices, stir, and continue to simmer for thirty minutes more or until mixture is very thick. Stir the butter from the bottom of the pan several times during the last five minutes of cooking so that it does not stick. Turn the butter into a small bowl. Serve at once, or refrigerate and serve when desired.

~ The Homeplace Recipe ~

Beaten Biscuits

3 cups flour   3 tablespoons cold butter
1/2 cup cold water   1 teaspoon sugar
1/2 teaspoon baking soda   1 teaspoon cream of tartar
1/2 teaspoon salt

Mix dry ingredients together. Cut in butter, add water. Mix to make a dough. Beat dough with a mallet for thirty minutes (300 heavy strokes). Roll to less than half-inch thick, cut in rounds, place on cookie sheet, and prick with a fork. Bake in a slow oven, 300 degrees, for twenty to thirty minutes until lightly browned.

~ The Homeplace Recipe ~

For beaten biscuits, beat 300 strokes for everyday biscuits and 500 strokes for company!

~ Southern saying

To Boil a Turkey with Oysters

This is an old fashion way of dressing a turkey,

but a very good one,

to those who are fond of oysters.

Clean and season your turkey as before directed,

and fill it with a stuffing made in the following manner:

chop fine twenty large fresh oysters,

mix them with a large handful of grated bread,

four ounces of butter,

a small handful of chopped parsley,

a grated nutmeg,

enough of the yolk of eggs and sweet cream

to make it sufficiently moist,

and work it with your hands until it is well mixed.

Skewer the liver and gizzard to the sides, the legs to the body,

dust and boil it as before directed.

Serve it with a boat of oyster sauce,

and have stewed fruit and boiled ham

to eat with it.

~ Lettice Bryan, The Kentucky Housewife, 1839

Flocks of wild turkeys abounded between the rivers in 1850. A mixture of meats in the pie is common in nineteenth-century cookbooks.

Turkey and Ham Pie

Makes one 9-inch pie (6-8 servings)

1 recipe pie paste for a double-crust pie	4 tablespoons butter
2 1/2 cups turkey broth	4 tablespoons flour
1 teaspoon salt	½ cup light cream
1 slice country ham, cut in 1-inch dice	Freshly ground black pepper
1 tablespoon melted and cooled butter	3 cups cubed cooked turkey

Make the pastry, and line a lightly buttered pie plate with one-half of it. Put the other half of pastry in a covered bowl, and put both bowl and pie plate in the refrigerator to chill while you make the filling.

Preheat the oven to 300°.

Cream together the butter and flour by beating and mashing them together with a spoon. Heat the turkey broth in a two-quart saucepan until it boils, reduce the heat to a simmer, and then begin to add the butter-flour mixture, one tablespoon at a time, stirring until the butter is melted. Continue to stir until the broth has thickened to a smooth, heavy gravy. Stir in the cream, the salt, and a few grindings of black pepper.

Fill the prepared pie shell with the turkey and cover the turkey with the country ham. Pour in the gravy. Adjust the top crust, brush it evenly with the melted butter, and cut two vent holes for steam to escape with the tines of a fork.

Bake the pie in the center of the oven for about one and one/half hours until the crust is golden brown. Cool for about ten minutes and serve.

~ The Homeplace Recipe ~

Many things from the nineteenth century are now extinct; we will never see a passenger pigeon, and it is rare to see an American Chestnut tree. In the early 1900s, a lethal fungus caused the blight on the American Chestnut, decimating large tracts of timber. The American Chestnut tree was an important food source and cash crop for people in the 1850s, but also a major food source for wildlife. American Chestnut was also prized for the straight-grained wood that was easy to work, lightweight and highly rot resistant. It was used from everything from fence post to musical instruments. Organizations like The American Chestnut Foundation and the American Chestnut Cooperators' Foundation, in cooperation with other organizations, are working to develop fungus-resistant American Chestnuts, so future generations can once again see forests of American Chestnut trees.

To Roast Chestnuts

…Cut a slit in the shell of every one to prevent their bursting when hot. Put them into a pan, and set them over a charcoal furnace till they are thoroughly roasted; stirring them up frequently and taking care not to let them burn. When they are done, peel off the shells, and send the chestnuts to table wrapped up in a napkin to keep them warm. Chestnuts should always be roasted or boiled before they are eaten.

~ Eliza Leslie, <u>Directions for Cookery, in its Various Branches</u>, 1848

Pigeons in nineteenth-century cookbooks likely referred to the once abundant, but now-extinct Passenger Pigeons.

To Roast Pigeons

Scald, draw and wash them very clean,

rub a little salt and pepper on them,

stuff them with a little grated ham,

bread crumbs, butter, chopped parsley,

salt and pepper;

spit, dreg, and roast them before a brisk fire

serve them up,

put over them a handful of grated bread,

with a few spoonfuls of butter,

in which the juice of an orange or half a lemon has been stirred,

and accompany them with stewed peaches or cranberries,

and green peas or asparagus.

~ Lettice Bryan, The Kentucky Housewife, 1839

Roasting sweet potatoes for dinner at The Homeplace is the simplest task the cook has: she covers the potatoes with ashes, covers the ashes with hot coals, and forgets about them until dinner time. Sweet potatoes also appeared on The Homeplace table in this sweet pudding, which does double duty as dessert or vegetable accompaniment.

Sweet Potato Pudding

Makes eight servings

2 medium-sized sweet potatoes (about 1 pound)
2 eggs
1/3 cup plus 1/2 tablespoon butter
1/4 cup brown sugar
2 cups milk
1/4 teaspoon allspice
1/4 teaspoon nutmeg
1/4 teaspoon salt

Preheat the oven to 350°.

With the one/half tablespoon of butter, grease the bottom and sides of a one and one/half quart baking dish.

Peel the sweet potatoes and grate finely. You should have about two cups.

Melt the remaining one/third cup butter and set it aside to cool. Beat the eggs lightly with a fork in a deep bowl. Stir in the brown sugar, the milk, the melted butter, the spices, and the salt. Pour into the prepared pan and bake in the center of the oven for about one hour, or until the potatoes are tender. Serve at once.

~ The Homeplace Recipe ~

Sweet Potato Pie

Makes one 9-inch pie (6-8 servings)

1 recipe pie paste for a single crust pie

3 medium-sized sweet potatoes
   (about 1 1/2 pounds)
2/3 cup brown sugar
1/2 teaspoon ginger
1/2 teaspoon cinnamon
3 eggs
2 cups light cream

Make the pie paste, press it into a lightly buttered nine-inch pie plate, and put it in the refrigerator to chill while you make the filling.

Peel and quarter the sweet potatoes. Put them into a two quart saucepan, add water to cover, and bring to a boil over high heat. Lower the heat and simmer for fifteen minutes, or until the sweet potatoes are very soft. Drain them and return to the pan, shaking them over the heat for a few seconds until they are thoroughly dry. Then mash them smooth with a wooden "beetle" or a potato masher. You should have about one and one/half cups of sweet potato puree. Set the mashed sweet potatoes aside to cool to room temperature.

Preheat the oven to 350°.

Stir the sugar, the cinnamon, and the ginger into the mashed sweet potatoes. Beat the eggs together with a fork in another bowl, add the cream and pour the mixture into the sweet potatoes. Stir until all ingredients are well incorporated.

Pour the filling into the prepared pie shell. Bake the pie in the center of the oven for fifty to sixty minutes, or until a knife blade inserted in the center of the pie comes out clean.

Serve warm or at room temperature.

~ The Homeplace Recipe ~

Gingerbread

Makes one eight-inch cake (nine servings)

3 medium-sized apples
  (about 1 pound)
1 egg
2 1/2 cups plus
  1 tablespoon flour
1 teaspoon ginger
1 cup boiling water

5 tablespoons brown sugar
1/2 cup plus 1 tablespoon lard
1 cup molasses
1 teaspoon baking soda
1/2 teaspoon salt
1 teaspoon cinnamon

Preheat the oven to 350°.

Grease the bottom and sides of an 8″ x 8″ x 2″ pan with the tablespoon of lard and sprinkle the tablespoon of flour into the pan. Tip the pan from side to side to spread the flour evenly and then invert the pan to remove the excess flour.

Peel the apples, quarter them, remove the cores, and slice about one/fourth inch thick. Spread them in the bottom of the pan and sprinkle them with three tablespoons of the brown sugar.

Cream the lard and the remaining sugar together until they are light and fluffy. Beat in the egg. Combine the flour, soda, salt, ginger, and cinnamon in a bowl. Stir together the molasses and the boiling water in another bowl.

Beat into the lard-sugar mixture one-third of the flour mixture, and when it is well incorporated, add one-third of the molasses mixture. Repeat twice more, alternating the flour and liquid in equal amounts.

Pour the batter into the prepared pan. Bake in the middle of the oven for about thirty five minutes, or until the blade of a knife inserted into the center of the cake comes out clean and dry. Cut into squares and serve at once.

~ The Homeplace Recipe ~

Christmas Ornament Gingerbread

Makes approximately ten large figures

1 cup unsalted butter, softened
1 cup dark brown sugar
3 eggs, well beaten
1 1/2 cups molasses

6 cups unbleached flour
1 1/2 teaspoons ginger
2 1/2 teaspoons salt
1 1/2 teaspoons baking soda
1 teaspoon cinnamon

Grease cookie sheets. Preheat oven to 350 degrees. In a large mixing bowl, cream the butter and add the brown sugar, eggs and molasses. Shift together all the dry ingredients and add them to the butter mixture. Mix thoroughly and chill well before rolling out on the floured slab. Cut the desired ornaments into shapes eight to twelve inches high. Use large cookie cutters or make your pattern from heavy cardboard. If you want to make ribbon hangers, cut a small hole near the top of each ornament. (You will tie the ribbons on after the ornaments have been baked and cooled.) Place the cookies on the greased cookie sheets and bake them in the preheated oven for twenty to thirty minutes or until the gingerbread is very hard.

~ The Homeplace Recipe ~

Christmas trees were decorated with homemade decorations such as the gingerbread ornaments, paper cornucopias, and gilded nuts. Germanic in origin, there are stories that the first American Christmas trees were from Hessian soldiers during the Revolutionary War. Christmas trees became popular in both England and the United States under the reign of Britain's Queen Victoria. Because there were so many American evergreens available, the Christmas tree became even more popular in the United States than in England. Both English and American Christmas trees were originally displayed on a table rather than on the floor.

Raisin Pie

2 cups milk
3/4 cup sugar
   and 3 tablespoons sugar
3 tablespoons flour
3 eggs, separated
2 tablespoons butter
1 teaspoon vanilla
1 1/2 teaspoons vinegar
1 cup raisins

Beat the egg yolks and add butter. Mix flour with sugar and add to egg mixture. Add milk and mix well. Add vinegar and mix. Cook over low heat, stirring constantly when mixture begins to thicken, add butter. Remove from heat when thickened and add 1 cup raisins and vanilla. Put in baked pie shell. Beat egg whites until soft peaked; add 3 tablespoons sugar and beat well. Pour on top of filling and bake until lightly browned.

~ The Homeplace Recipe ~

To Make Mince Pies

Take beef tongue, weighing about three pounds,

cut off the root, wash it

perfectly clean, and boil it till it becomes tender;

skin it, and when cold, chop it very finely.

Or, if preferred, three pounds of the inside of a

sirloin of beef, boiled till it becomes tender,

and chopped finely as the other. Mince, as small as possible,

two pounds of fresh beef suet; two pounds of currants,

nicely picked, washed, rubbed and dried at the fire;

two dozen large apples, pared and chopped very fine;

one pound of good brown sugar; sift half an ounce of mace,

and a quarter of an ounce of cloves; grate in two nutmegs.

The grated rind and juice of a large lemon

may be added, with a little citron.

Put all together into large pan,

and mix it well together with help a pint of good French brandy,

and if not moist enough, good sweet cider my be added.

Put it down close into a jar, covered closely,

and it will be good four months.

When you make your pies, take small round dishes,

or soup –plates; lay a thin crust all over them, put in your meat,

lay over the crust, and bake them nicely.

These pies eat finely cold. If the meat is not used immediately,

the apples had better not be put in until wanted.

~ Phineas Thornton, The Southern Gardener and Receipt Book, 1845

The custom of eating mince pies at Christmas, like that of plumb puddings, was too firmly rooted for the "Pilgrim fathers" to abolish; so it would be vain for me to attempt it….but I may be allowed to hope that during the remainder of the year, this rich, expensive, and exceedingly unhealthy diet will be used very sparingly by all who wish to enjoy sound sleep or pleasant dreams.

The dyspeptic should always avoid them as he would his bane, and for children they should be forbidden food; so tempting is the taste, that the only security consists in not tasting. So the "good housekeeper" will be careful not to place the temptation too often before her family.

~ Sarah Josepha Hale, <u>The Good Housekeeper: The Way to Live Well, and to Be Well While We Live</u>, 1841

Pumpkin Pie

3/4 cup brown sugar
1/2 teaspoon salt
1 1/3 cup milk
1 teaspoon cinnamon
dash nutmeg

1 tablespoon flour
1 1/2 cup pumpkin
1 egg, slightly beaten
1/2 teaspoon ginger

Mix all ingredients well. Pour into an unbaked pie crust. Bake in a 350 degree oven for 30 minutes or until set. Be careful not to burn crust (foil covering cooked crust or a pie ring will keep crust from burning while rest of pie bakes).

~ The Homeplace Recipe ~

Pumpkin Bread

(A sponge is 1/4 cup warm water and sugar and is made to proof the yeast to make sure it is active.)

The pumpkin first deprived of the rind, and afterward cut up in slices and boil; when soft enough it is strained through a colander, and mashed up very fine. In this state it may be used in pies, or mixed with flour for pudding, cake, etc. If it be intended for bread, it will be mixed with wheatened flour in proportion of one third to half. The sponge must be first set in the ordinary way with yeast in the flour, and pumpkin worked in as it begins to rise: use as much pumpkin as will bring the dough to a proper degree of stiffness without water. Care should be taken that the pumpkin is not so hot as to scald the leaven. It requires more baking than bread made entirely of wheat.

~ Thornton, Phineas, <u>The Southern Gardener and Receipt Book</u>, 1845

Christmas Candy

Fudge

2 cups sugar
1/2 cup cream
1 teaspoon vanilla

1/2 cup milk
2 heaping tablespoons cocoa
pinch of salt

In large saucepan, mix sugar, cocoa, and salt. Add milk and cream. Stir well. Cook over medium heat until a small piece of the candy dropped in cold water forms a firm ball. Add vanilla and nuts. Beat all until the mixture begins to thicken. Pour into a buttered dish. Cut into serving pieces after fully set.

~ The Homeplace Recipe ~

Cream Candy

recipe transcribed from local oral tradition

3 cups sugar
1/2 pint whipping cream
1/2 cup water
1 scant teaspoon salt
1 to 2 teaspoons butter

Mix all ingredients in a heavy 4-quart saucepan. Butter the marble slab or plate on which you will pour the cooked mixture. Cook without stirring until candy comes to hardball stage (254 degrees on candy thermometer). Pour on buttered marble slab or chilled plate. If you want vanilla flavoring, put it on the buttered slab or plate and carefully knead it into the candy. When cool enough to pull, pick up and pull until gloss dulls. Twist candy in long pieces and cut with scissors. Lay on waxed paper and set out until it creams.

~ The Homeplace Recipe ~

Taffy Candy

2 cups sugar
1/2 cup water
1/2 cup vinegar
1 to 2 teaspoons butter

Combine ingredients in medium to large saucepan and cook slowly until the sugar has dissolved. Then cook more rapidly until a small piece of the candy dropped in cold water forms a firm ball. The candy should crack when hit on the edge of a cup. Add a few drops of flavoring (vanilla or other flavors). Pour the candy onto a buttered plate as soon as possible. It is important not to scrape the pan while pouring the mixture, as hard pieces of sugar granules will form on the sides of the pan; if scraped into the mixture, it will leave hard bits in the candy. Work the cooled edges into the center with buttered fingers long before it is cool enough to pick up. When cool enough, pull the mixture with both hands, pulling apart and then bringing back together. Use fingertips as much as possible and work air in and out.

~ The Homeplace Recipe ~

Taffy Candy 2

Fill saucepan half full of coarse brown sugar, moisten it with molasses; add a tablespoon of butter and some lemon juice and peel; boil your candy and pour it on well-buttered tin sheets or plate; it must be very thin.

~ The Homeplace Recipe ~

'Twas the night before Christmas, when all through the house

Not a creature was stirring, not even a mouse;

The stockings were hung by the chimney with care,

In hopes that St. Nicholas soon would be there;

The children were nestled all snug in their beds,

While visions of sugar-plums danced in their heads...

~ Clement C. Moore, published in 1823 as
"A Visit from St. Nicholas,"
title changed in 1851 to
"'Twas the Night Before Christmas"

Sugarplums

3/4 cup chopped nuts (mixed nuts, mostly walnuts)
1/2 cup chopped raisins
1/2 cup chopped, dried apples
2 tablespoons fresh orange juice
1 tablespoon pear preserves
1/4 teaspoon ground cinnamon
1/8 teaspoon ground cloves
1/3 cup sugar

Mix all ingredients, except sugar. Mix well until the mixture begins to clump. Scoop up a small amount of the mixture and roll into a ball in your hand. Roll the ball in sugar and place on wax-covered plate or pan. Refrigerate until serving.

~ The Homeplace Recipe ~

There are not actual plums in sugarplums, though the size and shape of the candy is plum-like.

A Plain Plum Pudding

Pick, wash and boil half a pint of rice in a quart of sweet milk.

When it is tender, stir in two ounces of butter to cool,

adding a wine glass of white wine, one of brandy,

a powdered nutmeg and a tea-spoonful of cinnamon.

Having picked, washed and dried a pound of currants,

dredge them lightly with flour, and beat to a froth six fresh eggs;

stir them alternately and very gradually into the mixture,

giving it a hard stirring at the last.

Put it into a buttered dish, bake it in a moderate oven, and

grate loaf sugar over it when cold.

~ Lettice Bryan, <u>The Kentucky Housewife</u>,1839

A tradition called "The Family Stirabout" was practiced in Victorian days. Each member of the family took a turn stirring the plum pudding and made a wish while stirring. It was believed that a wish made while stirring the pudding would come true.

> Cooks in the 1800s devised ingenious methods for using up leftovers: "gathering up the fragments," Lydia Marie Child called it in her 1833 cookbook, <u>The Frugal Housewife</u>.

❖ *I feel very unsettled, holidays spoil me.*

~ December 27, 1859, Diary of Jane M. Jones

Second Day Pudding

Makes six servings

1/2 teaspoons softened butter
2 eggs
2 cups milk
3 tablespoons brown sugar
1 tablespoon apple cider vinegar
1/4 teaspoon salt
3 cups coarsely crumbled gingerbread
1 cup finely diced fresh apple, or 1/3 cup chopped dried fruit

Preheat oven to 350°.

With the butter, grease the bottom and sides of a 1-quart baking dish. Beat the eggs with a wire whisk until they are frothy. Add the milk, the brown sugar, the vinegar, and the salt, and stir until all ingredients are thoroughly combined. Stir in the crumbled cake and the apple.

Pour the mixture into the prepared pan and bake in the center of the oven for 35-40 minutes, or until the pudding no longer wobbles when the dish is gently shaken.

Serve warm or cold, with a custard sauce.

~ The Homeplace Recipe ~

❖　*…Wool to knit, Lon & me some stockings commence…
have peafowl for dinner.*

~ February 5, 1859, Diary of Betty Gleaves

Making a Wonder Ball

An American Victorian Christmas gift was a wonder ball. The wonder ball was made by unraveling a ball of yarn and then rewinding it with the addition of little gifts added as the ball was rewound. As the yarn was used up in knitting, the gifts were revealed.

Notes for Your Homeplace

❖ *All hands busy fixing for Christmas.*

      ~ December 24, 1859, Diary of Jane M. Jones

Author's Note on diaries and recipes:

Diaries of farmwives from yeoman farm families of The Homeplace period of the 1850s are rare. The two women's diaries referred to in <u>The Homeplace History and Receipt Book</u> are examples of the daily lives of Tennessee farm women of this time. The diaries are archived in the Tennessee State Library and Archives. Also archived at the Tennessee State Library and Archives is the Journal (diary) of Samuel Stacker (Journal at Ever Green Farm). Though a wealthier landowner than the yeoman farmers at The Homeplace, Samuel's diary adds a man's viewpoint on farming in The Homeplace area in the 1850s. W. Williams' letters from Dover, Tennessee, from the 1800s were also useful.

To make some of the diary entries from Jane M. Jones and Betty Gleaves and Samuel Stacker more readable, I have made a few very small changes in punctuation.

The Homeplace recipes are both taken directly from nineteenth-century cookbooks and developed at The Homeplace itself from such cookbooks and regional recipes, using traditional methods of nineteenth-century preparation as possible.

In the historic recipes, primarily from Lettice Bryan's <u>Kentucky Housewife</u>, published in 1839, the recipes reminded me so much of poems, I could almost hear Lettice reading them to me. I have therefore broken the lines for the recipes into lines as I "heard" them.

Measurement and Temperature Conversions

Measurements

1 wineglass = 1/4 cup
1 tumbler = 1 cup
1 gill/jill = 1/4 cup
4 salt spoons = 1 teaspoon
1 small pinch = 1/8 teaspoon
3 teaspoon = 1 tablespoon
1 dessert spoon = 2 teaspoons
1 small teacup = 1/2 cup
1 large teacup = 1 cup
1 small coffee cup = 3/4 cup

Butter measurement:

The size of a…
    Filbert = 1 teaspoon, rounded
    Hazelnut = 1 teaspoon, rounded
    Butternut = 2 teaspoons, rounded
    Walnut = 1 tablespoon
    Hen's egg = 1/4 cup

Flour and sugar:

1 pound flour = 4 cups
1 pound white sugar = 2 cups
1 pound confectioner's sugar = 2 1/2 cups
1 pound brown sugar = 2 1/4 cups

Oven Temperatures

Very slow oven	250-275 degrees
Slow	300-325 degrees
Moderate	350-375 degrees
Hot (quick)	400-450 degrees
Very hot	475 degrees

How to Test Temperature of a Wood Stove with Flour

Spread flour over a small pie plate

and place it in the middle rack of the oven;

watch the following table of time.

If in 3 minutes:

The flour turns black, the oven is hot - 450 degrees.

If it turns dark brown, the oven is quick - 400 degrees.

If it turns brown as a filbert (hazelnut), the oven is moderate - 350 degrees.

If it turns light brown, the oven is slow - 300 degrees.

If it merely tans, the oven is very slow - 250-275 degrees.

Bibliography

Books

Alvey, R. Gerald. *Kentucky Folklore.* Lexington, Kentucky: The University Press of Kentucky, 1989.

Anderson, Janet Alm. *A Taste of Kentucky.* Lexington, Kentucky: The University Press of Kentucky, 1986.

Arnow, Harriet. *Flowering of the Cumberland.* New York: Macmillan, 1963.

Beecher, Catherine E. *A Treatise on Domestic Economy, For the Use of Young Ladies at Home.* Boston: T.H. Webb, 1842.

Berzok, Linda Murray. *American Indian Food.* Westport, Connecticut: Greenwood Press, 2005.

Botkin, B.A., ed. *A Treasury of Southern Folklore.* New York: Crown Publishers, 1949.

Braden, Donna R. and Henry Ford Museum and Greenfield Village. Dearborn, Michigan: Henry Ford Museum & Greenfield Village, 1988.

Breathnach, Sarah Ban. *Mrs. Sharp's Traditions: Reviving Victorian Celebrations of Comfort & Joy.* New York: Scribner/ Simple Abundance Press, 2001.

Brown, John Hull. *Early American Beverages.* Japan: Charles E. Tuttle Co., Inc., 1966.

Bryan, Lettice. *The Kentucky Housewife.* Cincinnati: Shepard & Stearns, 1839.

Buist, Robert. *The Family Kitchen Gardener.* New York: J.C Riker, 1847.

Cannon, Poppy, and Patricia Brooks. *The Presidents' Cookbook.* Funk & Wagnalls, 1968.

Child, Lydia Marie. *The American Frugal Housewife: Dedicated to Those Who are Not Ashamed of Economy.* (13th ed.). Boston: Carter, Hendre, and Company, 1833.

Cornelius, H.M. *The Young Housekeeper's Friend: or, A Guide to Domestic Economy and Comfort.* Boston: Charles Tappan and New York: Saxton and Huntington, 1846.

Clark, Blanche Henry. *The Tennessee Yeomen: 1840-1860.* Nashville: Vanderbilt University Press, 1942.

Clark, Thomas D. *Pills, Petticoats, and Plows: The Southern Country Story.* Norman, Oklahoma: University of Oklahoma Press, 1989.

Davis, Donald. *Southern Jack Tales.* Little Rock: August House, Inc., 1992.

Edge, John T. *Apple Pie: An American Story.* New York: G.P. Putnam's Sons, 2004.

Fraser, Kathryn M. *By the Seasons: Cookery at the Homplace-1850.* TVA's Land Between The Lakes, 1983.

Gehrer, Julienne. *Love Lore: Symbols, Legends, and Recipes for Romance.* Kansas City, MO: Hallmark, Inc., 1993.

Hale, Sarah Josepha. *The Good Housekeeper: The Way to Live Well, and to Be Well While We Live.* 6th ed. Boston: Otis, Broaders, 1841.

Hardeman, Nicholas. *Shucks, Shocks, and Hominy Blocks: Corn as a Way of Life n Pioneer America.* Louisiana State University Press, 1981.

Harris, Jessica B. *High on the Hog: a Culinary Journey From Africa to America.* New York: Bloomsbury USA, 2011.

Helton, Ginger, and Susan Van Riper. *Hermitage Hospitality: from the Hermitage Library*. Nashville: Aurora Publishers Incorporated, 1970.

Henry, Joseph Milton. *The Land Between the Rivers*. Taylor Publishing Company (written under contact between the Austin Peay Sate University, Clarksville, Tennessee and the Tennessee Valley Authority), 1970.

Hopping, Jane Watson. *The Country Mothers Cookbook*. New York: Villard Books, 1991.

Howland, Esther Allen. *The American Economical Housekeeper and Family Receipt Book*. Worcester: 1850.

Humble, Nicola. *Cake: a Global History*. London: Reaktion Books, 2010.

Kluger, Marilyn. *The Wild Flavor*. New York: Henry Holt and Company, Inc., 1973, 1984.

Leslie, Eliza. *Directions for Cookery in its Various Branches*. Philadelphia: Carey & Hart, 1848.

Luchetti, Cathy, and Carol Olwell. *Women of the West*. New York: Three Rivers Press, 1982.

Martin, Laura C. *Southern Wildflowers*. Marietta, Georgia: Longstreet Press, Inc., 1989.

McCulloch-Williams, Martha. *Foods and Beverages of the Old South,* 1913. Reprinted with a new introduction by John Egerton. Knoxville: The University of Tennessee Press, 1988.

Montell, William Lynwood. *Ghosts along the Cumberland: Deathlore in the Kentucky Foothills*. Knoxville: The University of Tennessee Press, 1975.

Newman, Richard. *Go Down, Moses: Celebrating the African-American Spiritual*. New York: Clarkson Potter Publishers, 1998.

Nicholas, Nell b., ed. *Farm Journal's Country Cookbook, revised and enlarged edition,* Garden City: Doubleday & Company, Inc., 1959.

O'Neil, Sunny. *The Gift of Christmas Past: A Return to Victorian Traditions.* Nashville, Tennessee: The American Association for State and Local History, 1981.

Owsley, Frank Lawrence. *Plain Folk of the Old South.* Louisiana State University Press, 1949.

Patent, Greg. *Baking in America: Traditional and Contemporary Favorites from the Past 200 Years.* Boston; New York: Houghton Mifflin Company, 2002.

Perl, Lila. *Slumps, Grunts, and Snickerdoodles: What Colonial America Ate and Why.* New York: Clarion Books, 1975.

Randolph, Mary. *The Virginia Housewife.* Baltimore: Plaskitt, Fite, 1938.

Rath, Sarah. *The Complete Pig.* New York: Crestline, 2011.

Root, Waverly. *Food.* New York: Simon and Schuster, 1980.

Southern Foodways Alliance, Roahen, Sarah, ed. and John T. Edge, ed. *The Southern Foodways Community Cookbook*: University of Georgia, 2010.

Spaulding, Lily May and John Spaulding (editors). *Civil War Recipes: Receipts from the Pages of Godey's Lady's Book.* Lexington, Kentucky: The University of Kentucky Press, 1999.

Stowe, Harriet Beecher. *Household Papers and Stories.* Boston and New York: Houghton, Mifflin and Company, 1896.

Sumner, Judith. *American Household Botany: A History of Useful Plants, 1620-1900.* Timber Press, 2004.

Thornton, Phineas. *The Southern* Gardener *and Receipt Book*, 1845. Reprinted with an Introduction by Shirley Abbott. Birmingham, Alabama: Oxmoor House, Inc, 1984.

Volo, James M. and Dorothy Denneen Volo. *The Antebellum Period.* Westport, Connecticut: Greenwood Press, 2004.

Wallace, Betty Joe. *Between the Rivers: History of The Land Between The Lakes.* Clarksville, Tennessee: Austin Peay State University, 1992.

Webster, A.I. *The Improved Housewife or Book of Receipts.* Boston: Phillips, Sampson, and Company, 1858.

Winters, Donald L. *Tennessee Farming, Tennessee Farmers: Antebellum Agriculture in The Upper South.* Knoxville: The University of Tennessee Press, 1994.

Websites

Alabama State Council on the Arts: *Musics of Alabama: a Compilation.* http://www.arts.state.al.us/acts/compilation/historical.html (accessed 2012).

Genealogy Books for Northeast Georgia. *Recipes from Old Newspapers.*http://fayestoneposs.tripod.com/id11.html (accessed 2012).

Greenburg, Hope. *Godey's Lady's Book.* http//www.uvm.edu/~hag/godey/contents.html (accessed 2012).

Library of Congress: *Today in History: January 8.* http://memory.loc.gov/ammem/today/jan08.html (accessed 2012).

McNamara, Robert. *Cards for St. Valentine's Day Became a Tradition in the 1800s.* http://history1800s.about.com/od/popularentertainment/a/valencards... (accessed 2012).

Moorhead, Laura. *Missing Drinks.* http://www.foodandwine.com/articles/missing-drinks (accessed 2012).

Stradley, Linda. *History, Legends, & Myths of Ices and Ice Cream.* http://whats cooking in America.net/IceCream/IceCream/History.htm (accessed 2012).

Vintage Cookbooks. http://vintagecookbooks.healthyeatingandlifestyle.org/index.html (accessed 2012).

Commons Wikimedia. http://upload.wikimedia.org/wikipedia/commons/4/43/Andrew_jackson_head.jpg (accessed 2012).

TOPICAL RECIPE INDEX

ACTIVITIES & ENTERTAINMENTS

About the Author

Geraldine Ann Marshall has published a number of books, as well as over 100 articles, stories, and poems (also published under Geraldine Marshall Gutfreund) for both children and adults. She is also a storyteller and tells stories at The Homeplace. She has a degree in zoology from the University of Kentucky. She has two grown daughters, Audrey and Rachel; and lives in a house in the woods with her boxer dog, Stuart Little, who likes to watch the wildlife with her. Stuart Little also likes to eat and sleep while the author researches and writes!

About the Project Coordinator
and History Consultant

Cindy Earls was raised on a small Pennsylvania German farm in a late nineteenth-century Victorian house in Southeastern Pennsylvania; she grew up surrounded by history and was taught traditional domestic skills. At an early age, she recognized the importance at preserving and teaching traditional skills and in her early teens began her career as a living history educator at Hopewell Furnace National Historic Site. After graduating from Pennsylvania State University, she moved to Tennessee and began work at The Homeplace in Land Between The Lakes where she cooked every day on the hearth or woodstove, recreated period textiles, and most importantly taught many visitors about nineteenth-century domestic skills and women's history. She is currently the Special Events Coordinator, but still teaches historic domestic skills in workshops and new staff.

About the Recipe Consultant

Charlotte Huggins is currently the Education Coordinator and living history interpreter at The Homeplace. She does historical cooking workshops on outdoor cooking methods. Many of her recipes are drawn from old family recipes. She is known throughout the area for her cooking.

About the Photographers

Jennifer Lee Roberts, currently a Domestic Coordinator at The Homeplace, has a Wildlife Biology degree and originally hails from Whitesburg in eastern Kentucky.

Some photographs by The Homeplace staff, as otherwise noted.

About the Illustrators

Brooke Gilley is currently a Naturalist at Woodlands Nature Station and uses her artistic talents to educate about nature.

Michael W. Earls is currently working on a degree in art. He has been drawing his entire life and has provided illustrations for brochures at Land Between The Lakes.

Friends of Land Between The Lakes

The Friends of Land Between The Lakes provide educational program services at the Woodlands Nature Station, Golden Pond Planetarium and The Homeplace at Land Between The Lakes. They also coordinate volunteer activities for the general public and provide visitor information services at five information centers. Additionally, they conduct funds development for projects such as the new Golden Pond Planetarium projector, telescope at the Golden Pond Observatory and the School Field Trip Group Program, which underwrites field trips to Land Between The Lakes for school within a 100 mile radius.

To learn more about Friends of Land Between The Lakes, become a member, or find out about volunteer opportunities, visit our website **www.friendsoflbl.org**.

We are a 501 (c) (3) organization, so your membership or donation may be tax deductible.

Contact us at:

Friends of Land Between The Lakes

The Land Between The Lakes Association

345 Maintenance Road

Golden Pond, KY 42211

Land Between The Lakes
National Recreation Area

Land Between The Lakes National Recreation Area, managed by the Forest Service, U.S. Department of Agriculture, is nestled between beautiful Kentucky Lake and Lake Barkley, offering unique opportunities for recreation and education. Whether you want to relax on one of these two enchanting lakes, camp with the family on a weekend getaway, hike with friends on one of our scenic trails, or plan a group wildlife viewing adventure, Land Between The Lakes has something you are sure to enjoy. We invite you to come visit for the day or bring your family and stay for a while. Be sure to check out our attractions as Friends of Land Between The Lakes interpreters bring the region's history, science, and environment to life. With more than 170,000 acres and 300 miles of undeveloped shoreline, let Land Between The Lakes be your getaway place!

For more information visit *www.lbl.org* or call 270-924-2000.

18915548R00149

Made in the USA
Charleston, SC
27 April 2013